THE LESSONS OF
AFGHANISTAN

The Lessons Of Afghanistan, War Fightin
60317

Anthony H. Cordesman

Significant Issues Series
Timely books presenting current CSIS research and analysis of interest to the academic, business, government, and policy communities.
Managing editor: Roberta L. Howard

For four decades, the **Center for Strategic and International Studies (CSIS)** has been dedicated to providing world leaders with strategic insights on—and policy solutions to—current and emerging global issues.

CSIS is led by John J. Hamre, former U.S. deputy secretary of defense, who has been president and CEO since April 2000. It is guided by a board of trustees chaired by former U.S. senator Sam Nunn and consisting of prominent individuals from both the public and private sectors.

The CSIS staff of 190 researchers and support staff focus primarily on three subject areas. First, CSIS addresses the full spectrum of new challenges to national and international security. Second, it maintains resident experts on all of the world's major geographical regions. Third, it is committed to helping to develop new methods of governance for the global age; to this end, CSIS has programs on technology and public policy, international trade and finance, and energy.

Headquartered in Washington, D.C., CSIS is private, bipartisan, and tax-exempt. CSIS does not take specific policy positions; accordingly, all views expressed herein should be understood to be solely those of the authors.

The CSIS Press
Center for Strategic and International Studies
1800 K Street, N.W., Washington, D.C. 20006
Telephone: (202) 887-0200   Fax: (202) 775-3199
E-mail: books@csis.org   Web: www.csis.org

THE LESSONS OF AFGHANISTAN

WAR FIGHTING, INTELLIGENCE,
AND FORCE TRANSFORMATION

ANTHONY H. CORDESMAN

THE CSIS PRESS

Center for Strategic
and International Studies
Washington, D.C.

Significant Issues Series, Volume 24, Number 4

06 05 04 03   5 4 3 2

ISSN 0736-7136
ISBN 0-89206-417-X

Cover design by Robert L. Wiser, Silver Spring, Md.
Cover photo: Northern Alliance soldiers carry weapons on the front line near
Zarkamar in northern Afghanistan, October 2001
© Reuters NewMedia Inc./CORBIS

Library of Congress Cataloging in Publication Data
Cordesman, Anthony H.
  The lessons of Afghanistan : war fighting, intelligence, and force transformation /
Anthony H. Cordesman.
    p. cm. (Significant issues series ; v. 24, no. 4)
Includes bibliographical references.
  ISBN 0–89206–417–X (pb : alk.paper)
  1. Afghanistan—History—2001– 2. Afghanistan—History, Military—History—
21st century. 3. United States—Armed Forces—Afghanistan—History. 4. War on
Terrorism, 2001– I. Title. II. Series.
  DS371.4.C67 2002
  958.104'6—dc21   2002012858

CONTENTS

CHAPTER ONE

INTRODUCTION

Historians know all too well that it is far easier to rush forward in drawing lessons from history than it is to validate them. This is even truer when the lessons must deal with something as chaotic as war. Moreover, the Afghan conflict is anything but a conventional war. It is an asymmetric war fought with radically different methods, by different sides with different goals and perceptions, and as a theater battle in a broader global struggle against terrorism. Although somewhat similar conflicts have taken place in the past—even the Soviet Union's experience in Afghanistan was different in terms of the forces on each side, the weapons used, and the alliances in the region—it is usually difficult to make historical comparisons.[1]

The problem of drawing lessons from the Afghan conflict is further complicated by the fact that the war is anything but over. The Taliban have been driven from power, but far more ex-Taliban have been dispersed than have been killed or captured. In spite of an ongoing nation-building effort, it is far from clear that the Taliban will not eventually resurface in some form. Furthermore, nation building in Afghanistan faces massive ongoing challenges that involve direct fighting among the various factions that once opposed the Taliban. Such factions already make active efforts to use U.S. and British forces, peacekeepers, and any other available tools to serve the interests of rival clans, tribes, ethnic groups, factions, and warlords. Even if the past fighting can be brought to a full halt, the ability to win any form of lasting victory in terms of nation building remains unclear.

Al Qaeda may have been defeated in battle in Afghanistan, but it too has had many fighters escape and disperse. Only about half of its senior officials seem to have been captured or killed, and the fate of Osama bin Laden and many others remains unknown. Al Qaeda continues to be engaged in sporadic clashes with coalition forces inside Afghanistan, and seems to have significant numbers of fighters in Pakistan in the tribal areas near the northwest frontier. Equally important, Al Qaeda had cells or associated elements in some 68 countries when the war in Afghanistan began. It has suffered major reversals in many of these countries, but it has scarcely been defeated in all of them. Consequently, Al Qaeda remains a global threat.

As for the broader battle on global terrorism, it has scarcely begun. There are at least 20 more movements that have threatened or attacked U.S. citizens in the recent past, and the primary area of such terrorist attacks before September 11, 2001, was Latin America. Several major states—including Iran and Iraq—are developing steadily improved capabilities to wage asymmetric warfare. Whether they deserve to be called members of an "evil axis" is debatable. Whether they are major proliferators is not.

There are good reasons why U.S. defense officials like Secretary of Defense Donald Rumsfeld and senior commanders like Gen. Tommy Franks have warned that months, and probably years, of fighting still remain. There have been many times in the past when states using advanced technology and conventional forces announced victory over guerrilla and terrorist forces, only to see these forces adapt or reemerge as a different kind of threat. Asymmetric wars tend to be highly adaptive; this war is both regional and global in scope. It is also a struggle that may come to interact with other conflicts such as the ongoing Israeli-Palestinian struggle and a possible U.S. effort to drive Saddam Hussein from power. Just as it is easier to draw lessons than validate them, it is easier to declare victory than achieve it.

CHAPTER TWO

DRAWING LESSONS WITHOUT HARD DATA

The Pentagon and the British Ministry of Defence have provided few meaningful statistics and details on the course of the war to date—only data on the numbers of forces involved, sorties flown, and weapons used—and the Taliban and Al Qaeda have provided nothing but systematic misinformation. Most of the manpower estimates available for land battles count the total U.S. and British forces in the area of engagement, not those actually engaged in fighting. Estimates of Al Qaeda, Taliban, and friendly Afghan forces—and their weapons strength—are little more than guesswork. Data released so far on Afghan casualties, collateral damage, weapons accuracy, and battle damage assessment are vague or self-serving to the point of being worthless.

Study teams like the Defense Science Board of the U.S. Department of Defense and the 35-person joint task force, Enduring Look, are just beginning to make a systematic effort to gather data needed to draw detailed lessons from this conflict.[2] As was the case in Desert Storm and Desert Fox and other recent conflicts, however, the theater commander prevented adequate teams of military analysts and operations research efforts from maintaining an on-the-scene effort during the most critical period of the fighting. This refusal to create such teams of experts may reduce some of the support and command burden during operations, but the resulting inability to evaluate combat activities as they proceed seriously limits the quality of

U.S. military analysis and is a continuing problem in the way the United States wages war.

There are some useful data on the number and type of aircraft flown and air munitions, and these data are particularly important in this war. From the initial phases of the conflict through the destruction of the Taliban regime, U.S. and British airpower played a critical role in each battle, in making the advances of anti-Taliban Afghan forces possible, in destroying enemy infrastructure and facilities, and in allowing the United States to use a relatively small number of Special Forces to successfully advise and train allied Afghan forces while targeting Taliban and Al Qaeda forces in the field. Since that time, the near total U.S. fixed-wing air supremacy over the battlefield coupled to the use of U.S. attack helicopters and heliborne air mobility have made it almost impossible for significant Taliban and Al Qaeda forces to concentrate and survive.

DATA ON AIRCRAFT AND MUNITIONS USE

The U.S. Department of Defense made the following sortie data available on U.S. air missions between the start of the campaign on October 3, 2001, and December 17, 2002, by which time the Taliban and Al Qaeda were already defeated as organized military forces. These data reflect the major role of airpower over the battlefield as well as the importance of precision guided munitions:[3]

- The U.S. Air Force (USAF) had flown more than 7,100 sorties, or roughly 45 or 46 percent of all sorties flown. The U.S. Navy (USN) had flown roughly the same number and percentage. Other nations had flown roughly 1,420 sorties, or 8 to 10 percent of the total.

- The USAF flew bomber attack missions, plus AC-130 gunship missions and a limited number of F-16 and F-15E missions, while the USN flew carrier-based F-18 and F-14 strike fighter missions.

- The USAF and USN have dropped a rough total 8,500 tons of munitions, or a total of 12,000 weapons, with the USAF dropping 6,500 tons or 75 percent (4,600 tons, or 72 percent, of which were precision guided) and the USN dropping 2,100 tons or 25 percent.

- The 7,100 sorties of the USAF included 450 intelligence, surveillance, and reconnaissance (ISR) sorties (6 percent), 3,500 refueling or tanker sorties (49 percent), and 3,150 bomber and transport flights (44 percent.)

- While the bombers dropped the vast majority of the 6,500 500-pound dumb bombs used, they also dropped roughly half of all the guided munitions.[4]

The Combined Air Operations Center (CAOC) developed similar data for the period between October 7 and December 23, 2001.[5]

- The United States flew roughly 6,500 strike missions and dropped about 17,500 munitions on more than 120 fixed-target complexes and more than 400 vehicles and artillery weapons. Roughly 57 percent of the weapons that were dropped were smart weapons.

- The USN flew 4,900 of the 6,500 strike sorties flown but delivered less than 30 percent of the ordnance.

- The USAF flew 25 percent of the strike sorties flown but delivered more than 70 percent of the ordnance.

- Comparisons of fighters to bombers may not be fair in terms of airframe-to-airframe comparisons, but the issue is mission capability and not aircraft type. The fact remains that so-called antique B-52s and B-1s based in Diego Garcia flew 10 percent of the strike missions but delivered 11,500 of the 17,500 weapons dropped—65 percent of all weapons dropped and 89 percent of all weapons dropped by the USAF.

- The 10 B-52s delivered most of the ordnance.

- The performance of the B-1 has produced contradictory reports. Some observers claim it did not prove to be as effective a platform as the B-52, and its low-altitude penetration features were not needed. Eight B-1Bs were deployed to Diego Garcia; one B-1B crashed into the sea on December 12, 2001, and the B-1B had experienced 14 class B and C accidents by that time. It had a rate of roughly one in-flight emergency for every three flights flown.[6] The B-2 had no class B and C accidents in fiscal year (FY) 2000, the B-52 had four, and the B-1B had twelve. Other reports claim the eight B-1Bs flew an average of four sorties per day, and its penetration capabilities sometimes were useful.[7] Other sources indicate that it has overcome its long-standing problems in electronic warfare upgrades and that during the fighting in Afghanistan up to June 2002 it delivered 3,869 bombs guided by the use of the global positioning system (GPS), with a mission-capable rate near 90 percent and a weapons release rate of 95 percent.[8]

- B-2s flew only six strike missions from the United States because Taliban air defenses were too unsophisticated to require the U.S. use of stealth aircraft. This too has produced contradictory reports. Some argue that the B-2's global strike capability shows the need for more aircraft, and Northrop has offered to sell 40 more for $40 billion. Other sources note, however, that each aircraft would still cost more than $730 million, that cracks were discovered in the rear section of 16 of the 21 in March 2002, and that availability was only 31 percent in 2001 and 37 percent in 2000 versus a USAF goal of 60 percent.[9]

- Bombers delivered the vast majority of unguided dumb bombs—roughly 6,300 500-pound bombs in loads of up to 20 per aircraft. However, bombers were also responsible for delivering about half of the smart weapons, including the GPS-guided joint direct attack munition (JDAM) that achieved combat circular error probable (CEP) accuracies of 6–10 meters and had a standoff range of up to 15 miles.

- The $14,000 JDAM was used at a peak rate of roughly 3,000 per month.

Table 1 provides detailed estimates of the number of sorties flown and munitions used as of December 31, 2001. Summary

Table 1
U.S. Aircraft Sorties Flown and Munitions Used in Afghan Conflict, before December 1, 2001

Aircraft	Strike sorties flown
AC-130	225
B-1	320
B-2	6
B-52	375
F-14	1,200
F-15E	250
F-16	470
F/A-18	3,700
Total	**6,546**

Munition	Air Force	Navy
AGM-65-G	1	—
AGM-130	1	—
AGM-142	2	—
BLU-82	4	—
CBU-12	977	26
CBU-87	164	—
CBU-103	573	—
GBI-15	2	2
GBU-10	13	—
GBU-16	—	274
GBU-24	—	34
GBU-28	6	—
GBU-31v1(JDAM frag)	4,083	—
GBU-31v3(JDAM pen)	509	21
GBU-37 JDAM	2	—
Mk-82	6,344	—
Mk-83	195	—
Mk-84	204	3,963[a]
TLAM	—	74

Source: William M. Arkin, e-mail to author.
[a] Almost all LGB or JDAM.

reports cover later periods, but they are vague about definition, date, and the exact period covered.

- Roughly 18,000 weapons were dropped by early February 2002. Of that number, roughly 10,000 were precision weapons, or 56 percent of the total. This compares with 35 percent of the 24,000 weapons dropped during the Kosovo campaign in 1999.[10]

- As of April 2002, 22,434 bombs had been dropped during the campaign in Afghanistan. Of that total, roughly 6,650 were JDAM munitions. Roughly 60 percent of the total munitions dropped were guided by lasers to their targets. In addition, as of April 2002, more than 22,000 air sorties had been flown.[11]

- As of June 2002, the percentage of precision guided weapons used increased to roughly 60 percent, and military officials estimated their accuracy to be roughly 90 percent. As of May 2002, The USN claimed that out of all sorties flown, combat aircraft had successfully hit at least one target 84 percent of the time. Additionally, the USN estimated that roughly 90 percent of the munitions it has dropped were advanced or precision weapons.[12]

- Although the AC-130H Specter and AC-130U Spooky gunships present during the fighting did not deliver high numbers of bombs and missiles, they were able to provide extensive combat support with 105mm guns and 40mm cannon. They have an unrefueled range of some 2,200 miles and, although they are vulnerable to air defenses, they have extensive countermeasures, infrared and radar warning, and flare and chaff dispensing systems (a key reason that the gunship costs as much as $190 million versus $30 million for a C-130H II). The USAF found the performance of these aircraft to be so effective that it is seeking to upgrade its existing aircraft and convert four more C-130H by 2005. The USAF currently has eight AC-130Hs and thirteen AC-130Us and plans to improve their air defense, fire control, cameras, and sensors and add ammunition racks. The aircraft will acquire all-weather combat capability and ISR links to allow it to be fully integrated into the U.S. net of other combat platforms and intelligence assets.[13]

The Defense Department did update its manpower and aircraft numbers data in June 2002 although it provided little detail. These numbers showed a total Central Command (CENTCOM) force of 55,000, with 7,500 in Afghanistan, 1,000 in Pakistan, 1,000 in Kyrgyzstan, 1,700 in Uzbekistan, and 13,000 afloat. In addition, the United States had 5,100 personnel in Saudi Arabia, 3,900 in Qatar, 3,500 in Oman, 4,500 in Bahrain, 850 in the United Arab Emirates (UAE), and 64 in Yemen. (The number of personnel in the Gulf dropped after April 2002 because of movements into the theater and because of cuts in the naval presence that dropped the personnel afloat by 9,000.) The United States had a total of 570 aircraft for the entire CENTCOM area, including the Afghan conflict; this includes 195 fixed-wing shooters, 40 attack helicopters, 125 support helicopters, 110 fixed-wing cargo aircraft, 40 ISR aircraft, 60 tankers, and 90 allied coalition aircraft.[14] However, there are still no meaningful official data on battle damage assessments or combat effectiveness and no reliable data on the use of munitions by type or kind of target.

The United States has not released the full details of its use of cruise missiles. The United States and Britain do seem to have fired more than 50 during the early days of the war, but the United States did not draw down heavily on its stockpile because Afghanistan had comparatively few valuable fixed targets and no effective air defenses after the first few waves of U.S. strikes.[15] U.S. experts indicate, however, that the cruise missiles with GPS proved to be far more reliable and accurate than the earlier design used during the Gulf War that relied on radar mapping and terrain features. Operational accuracies within 10 meters seem to have been common. GPS also allowed the cruise missiles to home in without having to follow predictable mapping corridors in restrikes against the same general target area. During the Gulf War, many cruise missiles had to fly virtually the same predictable route when striking targets like Baghdad.

COMPARING THE AFGHAN AIR EFFORT WITH THE GULF WAR AND THE BOSNIA/KOSOVO AIR CAMPAIGN

It is possible to make some rough comparisons of the level of U.S. air effort in the Afghan War as of early 2002 relative to the U.S. effort in the Gulf War and in Kosovo. These data are in table 2. Although there are some minor definitional problems, the data clearly reflect the relative level of the total air and air strike efforts and the steady shift toward the increased use of precision weapons. At the same time, note that key factors like sortie rates are highly contingency dependent, the target mix differed strikingly in each case, and no quantifiable data are available on trends in terms of the effectiveness of given munitions or aircraft. It is unfortunate that other data that have emerged on aircraft and munitions effectiveness are extremely impressionistic and uncertain.

COST ESTIMATES

U.S. Costs during Fighting

The U.S. Department of Defense has issued more cost data than military effectiveness data. Estimates of the cost of the war to the United States alone for Operation Enduring Freedom were $3 billion in early December 2001 and $3.8 billon as of January 8, 2002. The total cost—including mobilizing reserves, deploying U.S. forces to the theater, and flying air defense missions in the U.S. homeland—was $6.4 billion. The direct costs of the war in Afghanistan included $1.94 billion to deploy and sustain U.S. forces, including three U.S. aircraft carrier battle groups. It also included some $1.57 billion to pay for the reserve and National Guard personnel mobilized through January 8, 2002, plus $969 million on agency support; $372 million for munitions, including some 4,600 JDAM bombs and at least 95 Tomahawk cruise missiles; $383 million to replace lost equipment; $103 million to fly C-17 humanitarian relief missions; and $45 million for flights carrying equipment and supplies for combat operations.[16]

Table 2
U.S. Airpower in Recent Regional Conflicts

Characteristics of the air war	Desert Storm	Serbia/Kosovo	Afghanistan[a]
Area of operations (sq. mi.)	176,000	39,500	250,000
Length of war (days)	43	78	in progress
Total sorties during period reported	118,700	37,500 to 38,000	29,000 to 38,000[b]
Percentage of total sorties flown by United States[b]	85	60	92
Offensive strike sorties	41,300	10,808 to 14,006[c]	17,500
Sorties per day	2,800	200, climbing to 2,000	25, climbing to 200
Total bombs delivered[b]	265,000	23,000	22,000
Precision guided bombs delivered[b]	20,450	8,050	12,500
Percentage of total munitions that are precision guided	7 to 8	35	56
Percentage of precision guided weapons delivered by the United States	89	80	99
Combat losses	38	2	0

Sources: Significant problems of definition exist in making such counts, and historical sources differ. This count is based on the work of Thomas Keaney at The Johns Hopkins University, and Michael E. O'Hanlon, "A Flawed Masterpiece," Foreign Affairs 81, no. 3, March/April 2002, p. 52. O'Hanlon evidently reports on a longer period than does Keaney.

[a] Afghanistan data are current as of early 2002.
[b] Data are based on Michael E. O'Hanlon and an estimate of 38,000 total sorties flown.
[c] The USAF reported a normal figure of 12,600 "shooter sorties." See Anthony H. Cordesman, The Lessons and Non-Lessons of the Air and Missile Campaign in Kosovo (Westport, Conn.: Praeger, 2001), pp. 42–44.

Cost Cutting

One key feature of these costs was the fact that the JDAM—a $14,000 GPS guidance kit for conventional 1,000- and 2,000-pound bombs—regularly achieved accuracies of 6–10 meters and came to dominate the delivery of guided weapons. This sharply lowered the cost of precision guided and standoff missions. It indicates that the United States can develop a future high-low munitions mix that emphasizes high-cost and low-cost precision guided weapons rather than high-cost precision weapons and cheap dumb bombs.[17]

Homeland Defense

Homeland defense expenditures included $1.5 billion in pay for 63,567 reserve and National Guard personnel, $432 million for National Guard combat air patrols over the United States from 26 air bases on 15-minute alert, $362 million for National Guard and reserve lodging and travel, and $252 million for the health care costs associated with mobilization. These totals do not cover expenditures since January 8, and compare with roughly $1.7 billion as the U.S. share of the war in Kosovo.[18]

NOTES

[1] While the definitions of conflict and war have somewhat of a consensus status in international law, in practice the use of the terminology can be somewhat subjective. At the First Hague Peace Conference, held in 1899 with Tsar Nicholas II, delegates formally adopted the Martens Clause, which admitted the difficulty of defining and using the term "war." In 1949, the United Nations (UN) conventions clarified that absent a declaration of war, nations fighting each other are in fact engaged in an "armed conflict." However, as both public officials and the media have characterized the fighting in Afghanistan as a war, this analysis will use the terms "war" and "conflict" interchangeably.

[2] *Defense Daily,* April 10, 2002, p. 7.

[3] *Jane's Defense Weekly,* January 2, 2001, pp. 20–27.

[4] *Los Angeles Times,* February 10, 2002.

[5] See William M. Arkin, "Old-Timers Proved Invaluable in Afghanistan Air Campaign," *Los Angeles Times,* February 10, 2002.

[6] Also see *Aerospace Daily,* December 13, 2001.

[7] *Los Angeles Times,* December 12, 2001; *Jane's Defense Weekly,* December 3, 2001, p. 28.

[8] *Aviation Week & Space Technology,* June 24, 2002, p. 47.

[9] *New York Times,* December 11, 2001; March 20, 2002.

[10] Bryan Bender, Kim Burger, and Andrew Koch, "Afghanistan: First Lessons," *Jane's Defense Weekly,* December 19, 2001, p. 20; *New York Times,* February 8, 2002, p. A-14; and *Philadelphia Inquirer,* February 12, 2002, p. 1.

[11] *New York Times,* April 9, 2002.

[12] *New York Times,* June 25, 2002; *Aviation Week & Space Technology,* April 28, 2002, p. 55.

[13] *Defense News,* January 14, 2002, p. 28; April 29, 2002, p. 6.

[14] Public Affairs Office, U.S. Department of Defense, June 27, 2002.

[15] *Washington Times,* December 13, 2001, p. 7.

[16] Department of Defense figures reported in Bloomberg.com, January 22, 2002.

[17] For further details, see Bill Sweetman, "The Falling Price of Precision," *Jane's International Defense Review,* April 2002, pp. 46–50. The JDAM had an initial cost of $40,000 and a CEP specification of 13 meters. The cost is now roughly one-third of that and CEPs of less than 5 meters have regularly been achieved on test ranges.

[18] Department of Defense figures reported in Bloomberg.com, January 22, 2002.

CHAPTER THREE

A UNIQUE WAR WITH UNIQUE INTANGIBLES

A lack of hard data has not stopped experts from rushing ahead to draw dramatic lessons about technology, tactics, and future wars. It is important to understand, however, that there will be serious problems in drawing lessons from the present Afghan conflict, even when far better data become available. It is a unique war, fought under unique conditions, and it has involved unique political and strategic intangibles.

THE UNIQUE CONDITIONS OF WAR

The challenge for the United States and Britain was greatly increased by distance, a lack of prewar forward bases, major regional political sensitivities, weather, and by dealing with a dispersed enemy located in a country the size of Texas. At the same time, the challenge was reduced by a number of factors, the importance of which became steadily more apparent during the course of the war:

- The Taliban government was deeply unpopular, if not hated, by a large percentage of Afghans, including many Pashtuns. Al Qaeda was far more hated and seen as a foreign mix of Arabs, Central Asians, Pakistanis, and others. The Afghans may be a highly nationalist people, but they saw their government and Al Qaeda as "foreign" and oppressive.

- An organized and armed opposition with—by Afghan standards—extensive combat experience still existed in the country. Although the opposition was often inefficient and poorly organized, the Taliban and Al Qaeda were forced to disperse their military assets over a very wide area and often in hostile territory. Small numbers of U.S. advisers and small amounts of arms and aid could often decisively tilt the balance in a given tactical area.

- The air defenses available to the Taliban and Al Qaeda were so limited that an air force in Afghanistan practically did not exist, and Afghanistan's air force could not make effective use of its few remaining major surface-to-air missile units. It had little readiness and training to use antiaircraft guns and man-portable surface-to-air missiles. This allowed the United States to win near-total air supremacy early in the war and allowed U.S. combat and support aircraft to operate freely over the battlefield with only minimal suppression of enemy air defense (SEAD) activity. The United States also had freedom of action in using transport aircraft and helicopters and could take advantage of relatively vulnerable strike platforms like the AC-130.

- The Taliban and Al Qaeda were sometimes credited with having a force of up to 125,000, but fewer than 25,000 were serious fighters and their training was largely in light arms, artillery, and light infantry combat. The force had no real experience beyond line-of-sight target capabilities, no meaningful night vision capability, and no armored or mechanized units larger than battalion size. The largest operational element seems to have had fewer than 70 tanks.

- The Taliban had arisen as a largely urban movement and had little real experience in guerrilla warfare. It was heavily dependent on Al Qaeda elements and Pakistani military aid and had come to power by defeating warlords and a Northern Alliance that had already largely defeated itself. The Taliban had relatively little experience in maintaining, sustaining, or using modern arms.

- While the Taliban and Al Qaeda had comparatively few fixed assets and facilities, the assets it did have were critical to its ability to coordinate, reinforce, and support combat operations. It was heavily dependent on trucks and a small number of transport aircraft for mobility and sustainment.

- Exposed terrain, road-limited reinforcement and resupply, the inability to shelter among the population in many areas, and the need to concentrate armor and artillery for the defense of key cities and to fight major opposition elements meant that much of the key armor, artillery, land vehicle, and communications assets of the Taliban and Al Qaeda could be targeted day and night by aircraft, Special Forces, unmanned aerial vehicles (UAVs), joint surveillance target attack radar systems (JSTARS), and other U.S. assets. The lack of threat to U.S. aircraft meant that such aircraft could linger over the area and kill on a target-of-opportunity basis.

- The Taliban and Al Qaeda could not disperse or retreat without exposing their forces, and both United States and opposition forces could kill them from a distance without the Taliban and Al Qaeda being able to reply. Convoys could not move and survive; ground forces could not stay and survive; and the Taliban could not abandon urban areas and continue to rule.

- The almost mercantile character of intra-Afghan fighting and the fact that the Taliban depended heavily on elements whose loyalty was opportunistic at best meant that as soon as the Taliban suffered major defeats it could not hold onto many force elements; it also meant that the United States could outbid the Taliban in terms of rewards and power. This interacted with the ability of U.S. airpower to strike freely over the battlefield and the ability of U.S. and British Special Forces to call in air and missile strikes and operate with night vision devices and long-range reconnaissance and targeting assets like aircraft and unmanned aerial vehicles.

- Al Qaeda seems to have had great skill in making itself hated throughout the country and had to concentrate in barracks and facilities to protect itself. Its creation of cave and training-camp sanctuaries gave it some physical protection from air strikes but also created target complexes that were the equivalent of target zones or rattraps. Al Qaeda could not depend on support from the Afghan people, and Al Qaeda members were generally so isolated that U.S. ground troops could—in extremis—besiege or attack them without becoming involved with the Afghan people or the quarrels of various Afghan factions.

- All these factors combined to make the impact of a comparatively few U.S. attacks and bomber sorties uniquely effective. The United States was not forced to rush in massive amounts of land-based aircraft or build up massive combat air bases in Central Asia and Pakistan. Instead, the average of 60–70 sorties generated by three carriers and an average of 6–8 bomber sorties per day could operate in a permissive environment where they could target at leisure, minimize collateral damage, and achieve considerable lethality and psychological impact against the Taliban's and Al Qaeda's comparatively limited number of heavy weapons, fixed facilities, and major depots and communications assets.

- Factional competition and warlordism created a number of problems for the United States in terms of false information, competition among factions, and targeting problems. In several instances, U.S. and local forces shared differing visions of a military outcome, with local generals negotiating surrenders enabling potential Al Qaeda leaders such as Mullah Muhammad Omar to escape capture on numerous occasion. At the same time, it made it impossible for the Taliban to concentrate on the U.S. threat, to concentrate on controlling any one geographic or ethnic area, and to know which group it could trust. The competition among factions and warlords also often made them very aggressive in attempting to split the Taliban in given areas and in rushing into areas in an attempt to seize power and weapons.

- In practice, the inability of U.S. and British forces to rapidly deploy and sustain large numbers of combat troops was turned into an advantage. U.S. and British advisers and Special Forces could use local forces as force multipliers, allowing local forces to also be the primary combat force seen by Afghans. This avoided making British and U.S. forces appear as invaders, equivalent to the Soviet forces of the past. While some critics have said the United States and/or Britain should have deployed many more ground troops much earlier, the net impact of that might well have been to create the impression of an invasion, provoking a broad Afghan backlash and allowing the Taliban and Al Qaeda to disperse into the countryside in at least the Pashtun areas with far more support.

- All these factors combined to sharply lower the intensity of the fight on the ground while the Taliban and Al Qaeda still had significant, organized military strength. So did the tendency of the Northern Alliance and other Afghan forces to pause and loot rather than close in on the enemy. The opposition advance was largely one of air strikes, clashes, bargaining, and concessions, not conventional battles. In broad terms, bargaining and defections meant that this was one of the few wars won without major frontal battles.

- After the Taliban and Al Qaeda had already been largely defeated, the United States and Britain were able to introduce significant ground forces into the theater; at that time a combination of airpower, vertical envelopment, and light mobile forces could be rapidly deployed against any remaining Taliban and Al Qaeda fighters.

- The terrain advantage that the Taliban and Al Qaeda might have gained through the use of caves and shelters in mountainous areas remained a potential risk and gave Al Qaeda forces some initial advantages in the fighting at Tora Bora. At the same time, any use of such fixed defenses became something of a prison or a trap. Although weather provided some cover and limited U.S. and British air mobility, it limited Taliban and Al Qaeda mobility even more.

- The Taliban and Al Qaeda lacked helicopter and mechanized mobility of their own, lacked the air defenses to prevent vertical envelopment, lacked the sensors to extend their situational awareness beyond visual range and at night, could shelter in caves only by losing significant tactical capability, and could exfiltrate only by dispersing and abandoning their supplies and heavy weapons. It took several days for U.S. forces to adapt to the Al Qaeda use of caves, small fortified fire points, and ambush areas at Tora Bora; but Al Qaeda had no way to match U.S. precision guided munitions, area ordnance, and attack-helicopter fire with mortars, automatic weapons, and light surface-to-air missiles.

- Al Qaeda had attempted to acquire chemical, biological, radiological, and nuclear (CBRN) weapons but did not have such weapons in any form, much less in the strength that might have affected or deterred U.S., British, and allied operations.

- Although Al Qaeda and Taliban elements could disperse after their defeats in Kabul and Kandahar and after the Al Qaeda defeat at Tora Bora, this dispersal turned out to be so great that they lacked the ability to sustain more than minor harassment operations. Unlike other such movements that could operate like fish in a sea of friendly people, the Taliban and Al Qaeda lacked the popular support and shelter in most areas and were unable to retreat and hide after launching raids and small attacks.

Anyone who rushes out to draw dramatic lessons about the decisive impact of technology, new tactics, or the revolution in military affairs (RMA) from the fighting in Afghanistan should take a very long, hard look at this list of unique conditions. It is not that new technology, tactics, and training were unimportant. They certainly allowed the United States and Britain to win far more quickly and with almost no casualties. At the same time, the Taliban and Al Qaeda had many unique limitations and vulnerabilities, and it is far from clear that future opponents will have similar vulnerabilities, that airpower can be used with similar freedom of action, or that the United States can rely on allied ground forces to the same degree.

It should also be clear that the U.S. and British air, naval, and land forces involved could not have been nearly as successful if they had not been highly professional forces with very high levels of training, readiness, and sustainability. For example, the United States and Britain were able to project power rapidly halfway around the world and sustain a broadly coordinated set of air-land operations over a combination of Afghan territory, allied states, and the Indian Ocean—an area about six times the size of Texas.

The USAF, U.S. Marine Corps (USMC), and USN air units that dominated the fighting had an amazing safety record. They demonstrated an ability to operate in spite of much longer missions than are normal—U.S. carrier missions averaged more than twice the length of normal peacetime training and past combat missions. In addition, they demonstrated equal skill in executing parts of the support effort provided by refueling, ISR, and support aircraft. Although some fixed-wing and helicopter crashes did occur, some of which were the product of high pilot workloads and fatigue, the overall performance was excellent in spite of long missions, frequent refuelings, poor weather, and difficult mountain flying conditions.[1]

The ground forces involved could not have functioned as they did without highly specialized training and expertise in special operations, mountain warfare, and highly mobile combat. The intelligence officers engaged could not have been as successful if they had not had extensive experience in using and coordinating ISR and tactical and human assets and did not possess the skills necessary to use them to support coalition warfare.

It is easy to ignore such human factors and military professionalism in analyzing the lessons of the conflict and to focus on the new technology and "toys" of war. In practice, the same outcomes could probably not have been achieved with something approaching Gulf War levels of technology but could not possibly have been achieved without the Gulf War's high level of professionalism, tactical flexibility and innovation, and use of force elements with high sustainability and readiness.

THE UNIQUE IMPACT OF INTANGIBLES

The United States and its allies were fortunate in the way the strategic and political intangibles affected the course of the war. Political and military uncertainties whose impact U.S. and British planners could not predict when the fighting began nearly all worked out in favor of the United States, Britain, and the Afghan opposition:

- The sheer success and sheer brutality of the attacks on the World Trade Center and the Pentagon gave the United States a major psychological and political edge. The George W. Bush administration used this political and psychological momentum successfully. It did so without escalating the country too far by attacking Iraq and without allowing the Afghan War to become anti-Islamic. Britain, Europe, and NATO did the same. This mixture of a clear cause for military action and a high initial degree of Western unity provided intangible political and diplomatic benefits that were less available even in "popular" military actions in Bosnia and Kosovo.

- The Taliban and Al Qaeda were truly unpopular in most regions of Afghanistan. They could disperse in some areas in the East and Southeast of the country, but even in these regions they could not marshal widespread political and popular support.

- Al Qaeda and the Taliban had important fracture lines. The Taliban seems to have been dragged into the war by the Mullah Omar's allegiance to Osama bin Laden. Many other senior Taliban do not seem to have wanted to get involved, and the divided nature of the Taliban made it easy for reluctant Taliban to defect or simply disperse.

- While the Taliban did score some initial propaganda successes in the Arab and Islamic worlds, this sympathy was negligible compared with the sympathy given Muslims in Bosnia and Kosovo and compared with the sympathy given the Afghan opposition during the Soviet invasion. It is particularly striking that Taliban propaganda had so little effect because the United States and Britain were slow to organize their own regional propaganda efforts and the United States was suffering from considerable political backlash resulting from its alliance with Israel and the impact of the second Intifada. This provides evidence in support of an additional lesson—that the clash within civilizations, or given countries, is often far more important than any clash between civilizations.

- With relatively few exceptions, Arab and Islamic support for the Taliban and Al Qaeda remained at the media and armchair level. The Taliban's propaganda effort was better prepared at the regional level than that of the United States and Britain at the start of the conflict. Such propaganda played a powerful role, particularly in producing exaggerated reports of collateral damage and the number of Arab volunteers who had been recruited by the Taliban, but steadily lost its impact as the character and unpopularity of the Taliban and Al Qaeda became apparent. By the time the Taliban position in Kabul collapsed, any notion that this was a war against Islam had been dissipated by a series of discoveries about how the Afghan people viewed the Taliban.[2]

- Afghan factions fighting against the Taliban initially proved to be unusually intelligent in their opportunism and did not turn on each other in combat or in midvictory as they had in the past.

- The Taliban and Al Qaeda military forces proved to be even more poorly organized than the United States and Britain estimated at the start of the conflict. They were slow to adapt, innovate, and react to their acute vulnerability to airpower at a time when they still controlled much of the country and had many of their land forces still intact. They did not show the flexibility of forces like the Hizballah or Viet Cong—although these latter forces also often suffered major defeats before they learned how to adapt their tactics.

- The psychological impact of bombing and airpower is always hard to predict. Perhaps because of the overall lack of air defenses and the resulting tactical helplessness of the Taliban and Al Qaeda, the bombing seems to have had a major impact on their willingness to hold on to positions and fight.

- No one can predict whether tactical defeats will produce a sudden, uncontrollable, catalytic collapse. This is always a possibility, it is rarely a probability, and it is never a certainty. In this case, however, a combination of the military and political factors discussed earlier turned what had seemed likely to be a much longer campaign into a relatively short one.

- The Taliban and Al Qaeda initially attempted to defend themselves in areas where they were both unpopular and highly dependent on motor vehicle movement along a few easily targetable roads. Not only did the terrain and limited infrastructure restrict the Taliban and Al Qaeda options, but they also helped channel U.S. ISR efforts. There were only a few built-up areas to monitor; few roads; and few points of contact among the Taliban, Al Qaeda, and the Northern Alliance. This permitted optimum use of ISR platforms.

- Ethnic divisions, the limited number of Taliban and Al Qaeda forces, and their reliance on cities made it impossible for them to hold out long enough to exploit the Afghan winter and would have made it difficult for them to operate in the most affected areas even if they had. In any case, winter did not come early or have a major impact in most areas of operations.

- Although the Taliban and Al Qaeda attempted to shelter in urban areas and use the population as cover, they were still forced to locate in compounds and in targetable areas where collateral damage could be limited. As time went on, the Arab, Islamic, and European focus on collateral damage also became progressively less strident as the limited impact of U.S. air and missile strikes became apparent and most Afghans' hostility toward the Taliban and Al Qaeda became understood.

- The United States was able to and did stand aside from any priority to broaden the war and fight on more than one front. No major active support links emerged between Al Qaeda any other country—Iraq in particular. No major follow-up attacks complicated U.S. overseas operations, and the anthrax attacks in the United States did not challenge U.S. capabilities for homeland defense. What might have become a far more serious multifront war remained a single-front conflict. In retrospect, broadening the war to include Iraq does not seem to be a good idea and certainly is not a lesson of the conflict.

- Internal Afghan conflicts have a unique culture in which various sides and factions routinely bargain, change sides, or simply avoid fighting. Instead of fanatic opponents, or even normal loyalties, the Taliban forces often initiated bargaining the moment they came under serious pressure, and then they changed sides or dispersed. This made it extremely difficult to contain and defeat the Taliban and Al Qaeda forces in detail, but it also made it extremely difficult for their leaders to force any coherent or enduring level of military action.

- The leadership of Pakistan responded quickly and favorably to U.S. initiatives, and was able to exercise good control over Pakistani Islamic extremists.

- The Central Asian states were willing to support U.S. and British operations.

- Russia and China proved to be highly supportive, and Russia allowed the United States comparative freedom of action in Central Asia.

- Iran tolerated or tacitly supported U.S. and British operations.

A great deal of U.S., British, and allied political skill and diplomacy went into shaping these successes. So did tight management of the media information campaign, and the political skill of U.S. and British Special Forces and advisers on the ground. Success in dealing with key uncertainties and intangibles was earned and was not simply a matter of luck. Nevertheless, the United States and Britain were still very lucky, and it is doubtful that the political and strategic intangibles will be as favorable in future conflicts.

The United States and Britain cannot count on such conditions and on such success in dealing with intangibles again. They are unlikely to approach the favorable conditions they encountered in the Afghan conflict unless they give equal importance to diplomacy, local politics, global and regional political sensitivities, and the need to build flexible and adaptive coalitions. Like the professionalism and readiness discussed earlier, these dimensions of war proved to be vital. Improved technology did not.

NOTES

[1] In many cases, pilot error may have been the result of inadequate avionics for mountain flying or having to carry out missions in very marginal flying conditions. One example is the KC-130 crash in June 2002. *San Diego Union Tribune,* June 20, 2002, p. 1.

[2] See the analysis in *The Estimate* 14, no. 1, January 11, 2002, www.theestimate.com.

CHAPTER FOUR

LESSONS FROM A PARTIAL VICTORY IN AN ONGOING CONFLICT

Given the background outlined in chapters 1–3, it should be clear just how speculative any attempt to draw detailed lessons from the fighting must be and why such lessons must be subject to constant revision. Nevertheless, some lessons can be drawn from our experience to date.

PROBLEMS OF DISTRIBUTED WARFARE

It has been clear ever since the battle of Tora Bora in December 2001 that even major military successes in Afghanistan may not have brought victory in any traditional sense of the term. This lesson has been sharply reinforced by the lessons of Operation Anaconda, which are discussed later in depth. It can be argued that Tora Bora was more a warning about relying largely on uncertain allies to carry out a ground campaign than a general lesson about the strengths and limitations of the U.S. approach to war.

Nevertheless, Tora Bora was the first major demonstration after the fall of Kabul that an enemy can disperse in ways that even the most advanced U.S. ISR capabilities cannot detect, characterize, and target.[1] The United States and its allies won the battle in spite of the problems of fighting against forces in nearly 200 well-positioned caves and fire points in the mountains. The United States and its allies also seem to have inflicted at least several hundred casualties. Nevertheless, the Al Qaeda forces largely escaped—often because Afghan troops either took payment to let them, simply chose not to fight, or let factional rivalries paralyze effective coordination and action.[2]

Nothing that U.S. and allied forces did in Operation Anaconda or in independent search-and-destroy missions, however, has shown that the United States and its Western allies have a solution to the problems of dispersed warfare against an enemy that is fluid and unwilling to fight. Al Qaeda has shown that it can disperse without a trace in spite of the best efforts of U.S., British, and Australian Special Forces; use caves and other hiding places to keep arms and ammunition in spite of massive search efforts; move into neighboring countries like Pakistan; and disperse into countries outside the immediate area of combat operations.[3]

More broadly, the United States has not succeeded in destroying the top leadership of Al Qaeda or the Taliban in Afghanistan. The bulk of Taliban forces has dispersed into the Afghan population, and many ordinary Al Qaeda fighters have escaped. It is clear that substantial numbers of Taliban and Al Qaeda forces have found sanctuary across the border in Pakistan. Lt. Gen. Dan K. McNeil, commander of the U.S. forces in Afghanistan, estimated that as of the middle of June 2002 roughly 1,000 Al Qaeda fighters still continued to conduct operations on or along the border area.[4]

Moreover, Afghanistan is only one country and its neighbors are only one place that Al Qaeda can operate in and disperse to. The U.S. Department of Defense has stated from the outset that Al Qaeda is based in more than 60 countries. Senior U.S. officials are still warning that Al Qaeda is capable of terrorist actions in the United States and other countries.[5] Senior U.S. military planners estimated in June 2002 that fighting in Afghanistan would have to last well into 2003 at a minimum. Months earlier, Secretary of Defense Donald Rumsfeld approved planning guidance for the period after the collapse of the Taliban that warned that the global battle against Al Qaeda and other major terrorist groups could easily extend to 2008 and beyond.[6]

Even the full defeat of the Taliban and Al Qaeda will not provide a firm guarantee that Afghanistan will not be a sanctuary for terrorists in the future. Mid- and long-term success in building a stable nation in Afghanistan is as uncertain as it is in the Balkans and all of the other countries where it has been attempted. In addition, the Taliban may rise up again in some form, or other warlords may offer sanctuary to terrorists. In fact, it is unclear that even a broad 68-country defeat of Al Qaeda would bring lasting victory.

Lessons for the Enemy

U.S., British, and other military planners and counterterrorism experts have already been proved all too correct in warning from the start of the conflict that the struggle in Afghanistan is providing lessons to enemies as well as to U.S., British, and friendly forces. They speculate that one key lesson for future terrorist and asymmetric opponents will be that they should create far looser and more broadly distributed networks and groups of cells that have a high degree of individual independence and survivability and that do not have a rigid hierarchy, a headquarters, and physical facilities that can be located and attacked. In fact, Al Qaeda has already shown it can adapt to U.S. tactics and intelligence-gathering methods by dispersing in Afghanistan and Pakistan and by constructing smaller, more concealed terrorist training camps that are not easily located by U.S. intelligence satellites.[7]

U.S. military planners also argue that key lessons from the conflict in Afghanistan to such enemies will be the need for more anonymity, additional emphasis on creating a cover organization and proxies, and the creation of a campaign plan of sequential or multiple attacks from isolated cells and elements so that no victory in any one area can halt the overall campaign. The classic case of Lenin's brother is a warning of what may come: the czarist secret police found and killed Lenin's brother and destroyed the organization of which he was a part. In practice, however, they may have done a great deal to shape Lenin's attitudes and behavior, causing him to become a far more serious threat.[8] More generally, other countries drew similar lessons more than a decade ago as a result of the Gulf War.

As the ground battles that followed the fall of Kabul have shown, the Taliban and Al Qaeda fighters remaining in Afghanistan clearly seem to have learned how to adapt their tactics in the months following the fall of Kabul and Kandahar, and how to disperse their forces in ways that make them very hard to attack. In spite of a major increase in the deployment of U.S. and British ground troops since the fall of Kabul, most U.S. and British land operations have not been particularly successful in finding the Al Qaeda and Taliban fighters remaining in Afghanistan. While special operations forces (SOF) can, in some instances, conduct operations in search of Al Qaeda fighters who escaped to or are operating in other nations in the region, senior military officials are increasingly depending on domestic intelligence and law enforcement agencies around the globe to assist in the search and capture of Al Qaeda members who have fled Afghanistan.[9]

Even though the United States may emphasize high technology and "net-centric" warfare, this kind of a loose, low-technology distributed network of fighters and terrorists may be able to present more serious dangers in the future—particularly in future wars where the opponent will be able to foresee the U.S. use of similar tactics and take suitable action before the fighting begins or before the point at which such U.S. tactics have a major impact.

It is at least possible that such forces can be organized to create a series of asymmetric attacks, phased over time, that would not depend on the existence or survival of some central or easily locatable command structure. Smaller, more conventional, terrorist attacks such as the car bombing of the U.S. consulate in Karachi, Pakistan, that killed 12 people have been at least financially linked to small cells of Al Qaeda and indicate that despite its fragmented command structure the organization remains capable of initiating attacks in the future.[10]

On the basis of interrogation of several Islamic militants detained along the Afghan-Pakistan border, intelligence officials now believe that Al Qaeda may be subcontracting smaller operations to local terrorist groups—providing them the financial means and expertise to carry out planned attacks successfully.[11] In the future, such a force could be organized to focus on the most lethal, costly, or disruptive means of attack and to avoid repeating past forms of attack. The lessons of Afghanistan and foreign war fighting cannot be decoupled from the lessons of the anthrax attacks on the United States and the possibility that a very small cell or a private individual directly attacked the U.S. homeland. The literature captured from Al Qaeda in Afghanistan shows both that it was aware of a wide range of U.S. vulnerabilities ranging from utility centers to the national political structure and that it had identified a wide range of methods of attack, many of which did not require large numbers of personnel.

Iraq and Serbia have already had considerable practical success in limiting the effectiveness of U.S. airpower by making use of surface-to-air missile ambush techniques, extensive force dispersion, underground facilities, decoys, and concealed supply depots as well as locating forces and facilities in civilian areas and using civilians as human shields.[12]

Note that a sophisticated military power like China fully recognizes the advantages of many aspects of the U.S. approach to warfare and is aggressively modernizing many aspects of its forces. At the same time, China has developed plans and doctrine to counter U.S. technological advantages and the RMA. China has paid close attention to Serbian tactics as well as Iraq's tactics in dealing with U.S. air and cruise missile strikes since the Gulf War. China feels that high-technology sensors, weapons, and nets can be countered through counterreconnaissance measures such as camouflage and concealment, decoy, dispersion, and frequent force movements. China too has emphasized the use of underground facilities, landline communications, and concealed supply depots. It has developed an air defense training team—Three Attacks, Three Defenses—that concentrates on attacking stealth aircraft, cruise missiles, and helicopters while defending against precision strikes, electronic warfare, and enemy reconnaissance. It also emphasizes speed, asymmetric methods, and preemption or surprise attack as ways of trying to bypass superior conventional forces.[13]

Ultimately, the Afghan War may give rise to a new cliché about asymmetric warfare: Short of a political and grand strategic end to a conflict, any given defeat of a terrorist or asymmetric opponent simply forces the opponent to adapt.

False Proxies, Black Flags, and Trojan Horses

Other aspects of partial victory need to be kept in mind in interpreting the lessons of the Afghan War. One lesson is that it remains impossible to prove a negative. Even in conspiracy theory, if it is impossible to prove that a nation like Iraq had some involvement in the acts of terrorism that triggered the conflict, it also remains impossible to prove that it did not. The same kind of uncertainties arose over Syria's role in the bombing of the USMC barracks in Beirut, previous Libyan terrorist actions, and Iran's role in the bombings in Al Khobar, Saudi Arabia. Nothing about Afghanistan indicates that the United States has found a solution to the state use of terrorists as proxies in asymmetric warfare.

This, in turn, raises the possibility that terrorist movements may deliberately attempt to falsely implicate states in their attacks and drag them into the conflict as allies or make them false targets. The same may be true of states doing the same with other states. One has only to consider what would have happened if Al Qaeda had deliberately tried to implicate Iraq in the September 11 attacks or if Iran had done the same thing. False proxies, black flags, and Trojan horses may become a major part of future asymmetric and terrorist conflicts.

USING NATIONS AS VENUES TO EXPAND CONFLICTS

It is uncertain whether the U.S. and British experience in Afghanistan provides lessons that can be applied with equal use even to relatively weak states like Yemen, Somalia, and the Sudan. If the fighting in Afghanistan teaches terrorist movements to use distributed warfare, they will steadily improve their ability to disperse and hide in unstable states. If they learn to use states as involuntary proxies, they will conduct operations in those states that attempt to make them targets, attempt to gain popular sympathy, and drag them into war.

A series of recent incidents across the Afghan border in Pakistan's western provinces indicates that Al Qaeda and other extremist groups are following this tactic. In late June 2002, 10 Pakistani soldiers were killed while searching for Al Qaeda fighters in the village of Wana, roughly 120 miles southwest of the Pakistani town of Kohat, which is reported to be home to several groups of Al Qaeda fighters. In early July, a shootout erupted between Pakistani security forces and a group of heavily armed Al Qaeda fighters at a security checkpoint. When the fighting subsided, four members of Al Qaeda were dead along with three Pakistanis. Both incidents occurred in a region where the Pakistani government has historically held little power.[14]

U.S. Federal Bureau of Investigation (FBI) intelligence information has confirmed that during the first half of 2002 several Al Qaeda and Taliban fighters who fled Afghanistan during the first half of the military campaign took up residence in several major Pakistani cities. These fighters have attempted to make contact with other militants who were previously trained in Osama bin Laden's terrorist training camps and may be developing plans to strike at U.S. and coalition forces in the region.[15]

Reports in the Pakistani media indicate that the central government has deployed up to 70,000 security forces, including 8,000–10,000 army troops, along the Afghan border in an attempt to locate and capture Al Qaeda and Taliban insurgents who entered Pakistan following major coalition offensives in Afghanistan. An estimated 17 U.S. operatives who are trained in the local languages and provide intelligence information on the whereabouts of Al Qaeda and Taliban fighters reportedly support these Pakistani forces. In addition, the United States recently allocated five UH-1 "Huey" helicopters to Pakistan for use in raids against suspected Al Qaeda positions. The concern among both Pakistani and U.S. government officials is that Al Qaeda may now be working with Islamic extremists in Pakistan to coordinate future terrorist attacks against U.S. and coalition forces in the region. U.S. officials are privately concerned that Pakistan has not fully realized the strength or potential danger to regional stability that the remaining Al Qaeda forces may pose. Eliminating the Al Qaeda and the extremist threat along this border region will be an important element of any long-term nation-building effort in Afghanistan and will be crucial to ensuring continued stability within Pakistan.[16]

Various other factions in both Afghanistan and Somalia have already attempted to label their opposition as terrorists or supporters of Al Qaeda and these factions have attempted to use U.S. and British forces as their proxies to attack their opponents. Indeed, Ethiopia has done the same thing on a national level in an effort to weaken Somali separatists.

Several incidents in Afghanistan involving the possible U.S. targeting of innocent civilians may have been triggered by rivalries between Afghan factions supposedly supporting the U.S.-British coalition. These include the U.S. attacks on two compounds in Hazar Qadam (in Oruzgan province north of Kandahar) on January 24, 2002.[17] Similar uncertainties arose regarding a U.S. air attack on a convoy in the area outside Khost on December 20, 2001, that the United States felt was hostile but that Afghans claim consisted of tribal elders.[18] Following an air attack in and around the area of the village of Kakarak, Afghan president Hamid Karzai publicly asked that the United States not launch a military operation based solely on the intelligence of local informants.[19]

Since that time, the United States and Britain have faced many situations in which military action had to take place immediately owing to the risk of losing the target entirely, but firm identification of a suspected Taliban or Al Qaeda target in time to strike a small, dispersed group of forces proved impossible. This has led to a number of suspected and confirmed strikes on civilians and friendly forces and the loss of substantial numbers of windows of opportunity. For all of the advances in sensors and situational awareness, even close monitoring with UAVs does not yet provide a basis for accurately characterizing small human and vehicle movements, particularly in nations that have heavily armed civilian populations and where males often move in groups isolated from women and children. Other sensor platforms designed to cover and target conventional forces—for example, JSTARS and various electronic intelligence (ELINT) aircraft—have virtually no value in such cases.

Repeating the initial U.S. and British victory in Afghanistan is one thing, repeating the hunt for Muhammad Farah Aideed in Somalia is quite another. What some analysts call "low-hanging fruit" may simply be traps where U.S. forces would have to wander off endlessly in search of enemies, alienating the local populace in the process.

Such risks will scarcely paralyze action against significant concentrations of real enemies, particularly when good targeting intelligence is available. Nevertheless, Afghanistan is scarcely a universal paradigm as to the ease with which such operations can be conducted because the U.S. ability to distinguish clearly between friend and foe has proved to be limited.

LIMITATIONS OF THE AFGHAN CONFLICT AND LESSONS FOR IRAQ

These factors provide an equally serious warning about going from the defeat of an extremely weak opponent, like the Taliban, to fighting a much stronger opponent, like Saddam Hussein's Iraq. Iraq is a far better organized, stronger, and more popular tyranny. It is also a power with modern internal security services, 2,200 tanks, nearly 400 aircraft, and heavy armored forces capable of serious war fighting. It retains an active air force and, more important, has rebuilt much of its land-based air defense net and has large numbers of surface-to-air missiles, radars, underground command centers, and redundant optical fiber command-and-control communications. It has at least some chemical and biological weapons and probably some surviving Scud missiles and extended-range Scuds.

If one consider the unique conditions of the Afghan conflict and the luck the United States and Britain had with several key intangibles, it should be clear that Afghanistan is not Iraq and that the military lessons of Afghanistan may at best have only limited applicability. At the same time, the fighting in Afghanistan also provides a warning about the dangers of putting too much emphasis on force strengths, military history, and the outcome of military analysis and of ignoring the fact that intangibles can suddenly and unexpectedly change the outcome of wars.

The size of Taliban and Al Qaeda forces—and the performance of Afghan forces in their struggle with the forces of the former Soviet Union—proved to be a poor measure of actual Taliban and Al Qaeda war-fighting capability and endurance. It was not possible to predict how long Serbian forces would hold out in Kosovo or to tie estimates of battle damage to either confirmed kills or Serbian political behavior. Similarly, the force ratios at the start of the Gulf War gave a greatly exaggerated picture of Iraqi military strength. So did Iraq's performance in the final battles of the Iran-Iraq War.

While the lessons of the U.S. and British military experience in Afghanistan do not translate directly into war-fighting experience in Iraq or any other case, they do show that factors like political and military leadership, morale, adaptability, and other intangibles could again lead to a far more rapid Iraqi collapse than force numbers would indicate.

The problem is that the uncertainties inherent in intangibles can work in two directions. They can also favor opponents. For example, Iraqi nationalism and Iraqi hostility to the United States because of the Gulf War and sanctions could work to harden Iraqi resolve and produce much stiffer resistance than during the defense of Kuwait. Events like the catalytic collapse of the Taliban and Al Qaeda were always possible but were not probable or certain.

As a result, the Afghan fighting has shown that U.S. air and missile power, intelligence assets, and targeting capabilities have become far more advanced than at the time of the Gulf War. The Afghan fighting has not shown, however, that the United States can count on its power, intelligence assets, and targeting capabilities to weaken Iraq in the same way as these factors weakened the Taliban and Al Qaeda forces.

CIVILIAN COVER, COLLATERAL DAMAGE, AND HUMAN RIGHTS AS WEAPONS OF WAR

Enemy use of civilian cover, manipulation of casualties, and collateral damage statistics is another lesson of the war. The Gulf War, the fight against Iraq since that time, Bosnia, Kosovo, and the Afghan War all saw efforts to use civilians and civilian facilities as shields against U.S. and allied attacks. Distributed terrorist networks and state-sponsored asymmetric forces can be expected to make steadily more use of civilians as shields and civilian areas as hiding places. Extremist groups like Hizballah and Hamas have gone farther, as have Kurdish terrorist organizations in Turkey: they deliberately blur the lines between the terrorist and combat elements and the religious, educational, humanitarian, medical, and peaceful political elements.

In the process, both terrorist organizations like Al Qaeda and states like Iraq have found that well-organized political and media campaigns can blur the lines of responsibility for terrorist and military acts, enabling terrorist organizations and states to use collateral damage and human suffering as political weapons of war. Wrapping movements in the cloak of democratic values, exaggerating civilian casualties and suffering, and exploiting human rights and international law are becoming a steadily more sophisticated part of modern terrorism and asymmetric warfare; so too, for that matter, are religion and ethnicity and the ability to exploit the causes and suffering of others.

Al Qaeda and Saddam Hussein, for example, have systematically exploited Islam, their identity as Arabs, and the second Intifada. Milosevic and his elite did something very similar in Bosnia and Kosovo, exploiting Christianity and their Slavic identity with Russia. The Taliban exploited the Afghan situation by producing grossly exaggerated claims of civilian casualties. Although an independent estimate by the Associated Press put the Afghan civilian casualty figure at roughly 500–600, the Taliban ambassador quoted 1,500, Al Jazeera gave estimates as high as 6,000, and one economist at the University of New Hampshire produced estimates of 5,000 and then 3,100–3,800. In some cases, the Taliban are known to have reported civilian casualties when there were no such casualties at all.[20]

Ability to Estimate Collateral Damage

The United States faces a broad challenge in dealing with these issues because it has no clear methodology for estimating collateral damage, detecting it, or estimating its scale. The fighting in Afghanistan has shown, however, that in asymmetric wars pilots and UAVs cannot firmly differentiate enemy forces and facilities from civilians, either in built-up areas or the field. The same seems to be equally true even of Special Forces teams on the ground. Independent teams cannot get the full background on suspicious movements and behavior patterns, and groups dependent on local allies often get misinformation or deliberate lies. Special Forces teams like Team 555 have demonstrated that groups on the ground can sometimes get information on the kind of unconventional combatants who fought in the Afghan War that is much better than information from any form of sensor or airborne platform; but no amount of fusion of data from combat aircraft, satellites, UAVs, SIGINT (signals intelligence) aircraft, and HUMINT (human intelligence) on the ground could fully characterize many targets or distinguish combatants from civilians.[21]

In Afghanistan a large number of civilian deaths have occurred not as a result of errant bombs but instead as a result of bombs accurately hitting their targets and destroying suspected enemy positions, but killing civilians in the process. By relying, in many instances, on air strikes instead of ground forces to destroy Al Qaeda positions, the United States has reduced its opportunities to verify the target intelligence being provided by local Afghan warlords. U.S. military officials argue that in many cases where the Afghans have said the target was innocent or that no hostile forces were present, the targets that were hit were legitimate; at the same time, U.S. officials concur that it is difficult to distinguish between civilian and military targets in built-up areas. Afghan officials contend, and U.S. officials dispute, that on at least three occasions the United States attacked villages and convoys based on poor intelligence from local warlords who were seeking to exact political revenge or gain political power. In addition, observers question the level of force that, in some instances, the United States has used to destroy suspected Al Qaeda targets.[22]

Although precision guided munitions are more accurate and less likely to stray from targets, the reality remains that they are only as accurate as the intelligence on the ground. During future fighting, the United States may need to revisit whether the use of air strikes to destroy targets hidden among civilians is the most efficient and least politically costly method of fighting the enemy.[23] This dilemma also reinforces the need to find ways of minimizing collateral damage in urban areas while trying to kill hard targets and attacking CBRN weapons and facilities.

The United States certainly seeks to minimize civilian casualties and collateral damage. Like other military powers, however, the

United States normally does not attempt to estimate either loss of life or the indirect costs of military strikes, particularly cultural and economic costs. Since the Vietnam War, the United States has avoided making public any body counts of either military or civilian killed. This allowed Iraq and Serbia to have some propaganda success with their grossly exaggerated claims of civilian casualties and collateral damage in past wars, and it has allowed the Taliban to make equally exaggerated claims during the current fighting. While many human rights groups have been careful to examine such claims, others have taken them literally; and hostile countries and political factions have done the same.

The United States was largely able to avoid the political backlash from civilian casualties and collateral damage during the Gulf War although exaggerated casualty claims—particularly relating to the "road of death"—were a factor leading to the early termination of the coalition advance and the early declaration of a cease-fire. Since that time, the United States has been less successful in countering Iraqi claims related to U.S. postwar attacks, in part because it has decided to address such claims on a strike-by-strike basis without addressing the details.

Both the United States and the North Atlantic Treaty Organization (NATO) had to address civilian casualties and collateral damage in Kosovo on a daily basis, and they often made mistaken claims or had to respond by admitting they were unable to confirm or deny many Serbian claims. This sometimes gave Serbia a propaganda advantage during the fighting although the U.S. Department of Defense largely succeeded in dodging the issue in its analysis of the lessons of Kosovo by issuing its after-action analysis only in a report to Congress and by doing so after the issue had lost major media impact. The Department of Defense also was able to minimize any potential fallout from reports of civilian casualties because it used a narrow definition of collateral damage that excluded many incidents. Data on Afghanistan are highly uncertain, but the following instances of collateral damage and civilian casualties seem to have occurred during the most critical part of the fighting:[24]

- October 8, 2001: bombs kill four United Nations (UN) workers in Kabul;

- October 13, 2001: strike by USN jet misses Kabul airport by a mile and resulting strike kills at least four civilians;

- October 16 and 26, 2001: Red Cross warehouse in Kabul hit by bombs;

- October 22, 2001: in village of Chowkor Kariz, AC-130 hits civilians who do not seem to have had ties to the Taliban or Al Qaeda;

- November 8–10, 2001: raids on Khakriz, north of Kandahar, attack fleeing supporters of Sheik Omar and may have killed 30–70 civilians (Taliban claimed 300 dead);

- November 26, 2001: bomb dropped on Qalai Janghi prison during uprising kills five Northern Alliance troops and wounds five U.S. soldiers;

- November 29, 2001: bombs hit civilian homes in Sanjiri, west of Kandahar;

- December 1, 2001: bombs hit Khazi Kariz, eight miles south of Kandahar airport, possibly hitting two civilian homes;

- December 5, 2001: Bombs hit friendly targets near Shawalikot, 21 miles north of Kandahar; Hamid Karzai, the 5th Special Forces group, and civilians in the area are hit by mistake; 3 Americans, 19 Afghan fighters, and an unknown number of civilians die; other strikes on Argandab and Sokhchala also seem to hit civilians;

- December 20, 2001: air strike hits a convoy near Khost; 12 to 27 die;

- December 29, 2001: bombing attack on weapons depot in the village Qualai Niazi kills civilians, including part of a wedding party;

- January 24, 2002: in Hazar Qadam, U.S. Special Forces kill 16–18; the U.S. Defense Department later admits the dead were innocent civilians targeted by a rival Afghan faction;[25] and

- February 6, 2002: Central Intelligence Agency (CIA) UAV fires Hellfire missile that may have hit scrap gatherers near Zhawar Kili.[26]

The most serious incident as of this writing took place in Oruzgan province on July 1, 2002. An AC-130 gunship attack on antiaircraft batteries killed a number of civilians, including a significant portion of a wedding party, in the village of Kakarak. The United States admitted to having fired on four villages in the area, and the Afghan government estimated that 40–48 people were killed and another 117 were wounded.[27]

Despite initial investigations by Afghan and U.S. personnel, it is still unclear what transpired. According to Defense Department officials, approximately 300–400 U.S.-led coalition and Afghan forces were engaged in an operation designed to locate and capture Al Qaeda and Taliban fighters still thought to be active in Oruzgan province, the birthplace of Taliban spiritual leader Mullah Muhammad Omar. Intelligence reports had indicated that "high-value individuals" were possibly "operating in the area." As part of the operations, a B-52 bomber dropped several bombs on cave complexes. An errant GBU-31 2,000-pound bomb missed its target and instead hit a hill. No persons, however, were injured as a result.[28]

U.S. officials have stated that after being fired upon and tracked by antiaircraft guns numerous times, an AC-130 gunship operating in support of the ongoing mission returned fire, attacking suspected antiaircraft batteries in six different locations. In the process, numerous civilians attending a wedding party in the village of Kakarak were killed and a larger number were injured.[29]

On July 6, the United States did acknowledge that civilians had died as a result of the raid in southern Afghanistan. After an initial investigation, however, U.S. officials were unable to find a large number of graves and are therefore unable to confirm the total number killed. No evidence of an antiaircraft gun battery was found in Kakarak although a truck-mounted antiaircraft gun was found roughly 10 miles from the village. According to military officials accompanying the investigative team, in addition to GPS and laser targeting devices, U.S.

ground forces could not confirm the existence of any source of anti-aircraft fire. The investigative team did, however, collect shell casings and shrapnel that will be analyzed as part of a large investigation. Because the AC-130 was equipped with a video recording device or "gun camera," the imagery it provides might assist investigators in determining what occurred.[30]

The U.S. Defense Department formally launched an investigation, headed by a USAF one-star general, to determine the exact sequence of events leading up to and during the incident. Afghan president Hamid Karzai has appointed Tribal Affairs Minister Arif Noorzai to lead a government investigation.[31] The UN also dispatched a team to the region of the incident to investigate damage to the local infrastructure.[32]

The Afghan government also responded by issuing its most vocal condemnation of a U.S. military mistake since the start of the war. President Karzai called on the United States and coalition forces to "take all necessary measures to ensure that military activities to capture terrorist groups do not harm innocent Afghan civilians."[33] Also, the Afghan foreign minister, Abdullah, called on the United States to reevaluate the procedure for determining targets and launching attacks: "This situation has to come to an end. Mistakes can take place, human errors are possible, but our people should be assured that every measure was taken to avoid such incidents."[34] For the first time since the collapse of the Taliban government, an anti-U.S. protest was held in the capital city of Kabul, outside the UN office.[35] Observers also reported increased levels of hostility among the ethnic Pashtun population of Oruzgan province toward the continued U.S. military presence.[36]

Despite the best attempts of investigators, the full details of this incident may never be known. However, it does provide further evidence of the limits and shortcomings of current U.S. ISR capabilities. Marine Corps Lt. Gen. Gregory Newbold, director of operations on the U.S. military's Joint Staff, notes that despite intelligence indicating the presence of Al Qaeda fighters and, possibly, leaders in the area, reports did not reveal that a large group of civilians had gathered for the wedding in Kakarak.[37] The incident also reveals the difficulty of successfully locating and capturing rogue fighters who can take advantage of the rugged landscape to conceal their movements. Highlighted also is the willingness of Al Qaeda fighters to locate mortars, antiaircraft batteries, and other weapons inside areas populated by civilians.[38]

In the aftermath of this attack, it may also be necessary for the United States to reevaluate its use of air strikes to destroy Al Qaeda positions. Strikes over such a wide area with such heavy firepower make it more likely that a significant number of civilians could be killed; yet some observers believe that, on the basis of current evidence, U.S. military officials failed to consider this before executing the attack.[39]

In other cases, it is unclear whether civilian casualties in fact occurred. The chronology of incidents scarcely logs high levels of casualties for a campaign that involved some 18,000–19,000 air weapons by the time the Taliban collapsed[40] and well over 22,000 weapons by the spring of 2002. In spite of some efforts by human rights organizations, there simply are no accurate estimates of Al Qaeda, Taliban, or other Afghan casualties. It seems possible that total casualties ranged from 1,500 to 3,000 by late December 2001, but there is no way to estimate such figures or to separate the casualties caused by factional fighting, warlordism, and banditry from those caused by the United States and its non-Afghan allies.[41]

At the same time, it is clear that the problem is real, and there is little reason to suspect that it will not be even more serious whenever the United States finds it must deal with more serious threats or more intensive asymmetric wars.

Designing Weapons to Deal with Collateral Damage

The other side of this coin is that properly designed weapons and targeting and ISR systems have already greatly reduced the problem of collateral damage and civilian casualties. The global reaction to the fall of the Taliban and Al Qaeda shows that the United States and its allies can continue to act in spite of enemy propaganda and the use of collateral damage as a political weapon, and that media and human rights criticism that ignores military reality and attempts to make any

use of military force impossible has little effect. The media and the public will—and they should—react to every attack that produces any form of civilian casualties, friendly fire, or collateral damage. If the world accepts the need for military action, however, it will also accept the inevitability of such losses.

The United States and its allies must, however, demonstrate that they have made a good-faith effort to minimize collateral damage and civilian casualties. Ever since Vietnam, the history of war has shown that each improvement in military capability is matched by demands for higher standards of performance.

This already is leading to steady improvements in weapons and targeting accuracy, the use of sensors to prevent attacks with high civilian losses and collateral damage, and new screening methods for target selection and strike authorization. The U.S. and British efforts to develop smaller precision guided weapons, like 250-pound versions of the JDAM, is one example. The use of precision guided small-diameter bombs (SDBs) offers a way to strike against roughly 70 percent of the targets that might normally be hit with a 1,000- or 2,000-pound weapon. SDBs offer a way to carry far more munitions per sortie, reduce the number of sorties required, or achieve far more lethality per sortie and still sharply reduce collateral damage. SDBs also can achieve ranges of 60–70 miles when they are launched at high altitudes.[42]

Miniature cruise missiles with multipurpose warheads, like the low-cost autonomous attack system (LOCAAS) are under development for the same reason, as well to improve the strike capabilities of weapons like the Predator and future unmanned combat air vehicles (UCAVs). So are so-called spiral SDB weapons that would have autonomous or optical sensors and search a wide area until they were homed in on a specific target.[43]

These advances are supported by similar advances in ISR capabilities. This is equally true of the series of major improvements in target selection and review made throughout the air- and missile-targeting process after the strike on the Chinese embassy in Belgrade during the air campaign in Kosovo.

Advances in accuracy offer the military the best of both worlds: more lethality but less collateral damage. And such advances can be applied to the delivery of unguided—dumb—weapons as well. UAVs and other sensors can greatly reduce the need to use artillery to fire into wide areas rather than at specific targets. The B-52s that dropped dumb bombs during the Afghan conflict made use of better navigation and targeting capabilities than ever before but also made the first use of the wind-corrected munitions dispenser (WCMD) in combat to deliver weapons like the CBU-87 combined effects munition (CEM). This is a strap-on $10,000 tail kit that allows for delivery with greater accuracy from higher altitudes, and it can also be used with weapons like Gator mine and the new sensor fuzed weapon (SFW). It scarcely eliminates the problems of using unguided area weapons, but it does reduce them.[44]

There are still areas where the United States can do more. British experiments with weapons designs that deactivate the warhead when systems malfunction or lose their targeting lock are one case in point. Another is the need to come to grips with long-standing problems in cluster munitions and dumb bombs that effectively turn them into mines when they do not explode. The use of improved release systems, navigation and targeting aids, and wind correction can help up to a point, but the United States dropped some 1,150 cluster bombs on 188 locations in Afghanistan as of early February.[45] They had many of the same defects as the weapons dropped in Vietnam and the Gulf War and often produced duds that could be lethal if handled or contacted. This is not a problem that should take three decades to solve.[46]

The Afghan conflict was the first time that the new CBU-103 cluster bomb was used. It is equipped with course-correcting tail fins that enable it to compensate for the significant drift that can occur when a bomb is dropped from an altitude of more than 15,000 feet. A new cluster bomb that has a small quantity of more powerful bomblets is under development. In an attempt to improve the accuracy of the CBU-103, weapons designers have incorporated into the new design a heat-seeking device that will allow the bomb to more closely track and hit enemy positions.[47]

Pentagon officials estimate that roughly 5 percent of cluster bombs do not detonate upon impact. The decision to package air-dropped food in the same color as cluster bombs further increased the risk that civilian deaths would result from unexploded cluster bombs.[48]

More generally, the United States needs to examine ways in which it can design its ISR sensors and systems, and its intelligence and targeting systems, specifically to minimize collateral damage and civilian casualties and to provide some form of near-real-time warning and/or imagery to allow rapid confirmation of whether mistakes occur. This does not need to paralyze operations; it means changing design criteria and methods to allow operations to be sustained with minimal cost to the innocent and minimal political backlash.

One longer-run issue that needs to be addressed is the need for some mix of methodology and technology that can produce meaningful body counts—at least over time. The disastrous emphasis on body counts in Vietnam—with its endless phony casualty figures and pressure to take risks in attacking civilian targets—is scarcely an example to follow. It is fairly clear, however, that if the United States does not produce reasonable estimates of its own, others will produce unreasonable and politicized lies. Beyond that, minimizing casualties does require an understanding of what casualties are. Physical collateral damage can always be fixed or replaced. People cannot.

Another task will be to sensitize the media and the world to the fact that the Taliban and Al Qaeda use of civilian facilities and populations to shelter their forces are violations of the laws of war. Like the Serbs and Iraq, the Taliban and Al Qaeda made extensive use of civilians and civilian facilities as human shields. The United States and its allies cannot prevent this, but it has to be clear to the world that the moral and ethical problem lies primarily with the forces that do this, not with the United States and its allies.[49]

CBRN WEAPONS AND ATTACKS

It is all too clear that Al Qaeda had a major effort under way to examine chemical and biological weapons and was examining nuclear terrorism in terms of power-plant attacks, radiological weapons, and crude nuclear devices. At least one general in India drew the lesson from the Gulf War that "no one should go to war with the United States without nuclear weapons." It is equally possible that terrorists will draw the lesson that if they can launch only one major series of attacks, they should not do so without CBRN weapons. States, on the other hand, may learn both lessons. They may see value in aiding proxies to develop CBRN weapons, and they may see acquiring CBRN weapons as a key deterrent to U.S. action in asymmetric wars. They may also see that the ability to launch on warning, or under attack, against U.S. allies and friends or against targets in the U.S. homeland will either deter the United States or force it to limit its range of attacks and goals in war.[50]

The United States still has not resolved the source of the anthrax attacks that followed the attacks on the World Trade Center and the Pentagon. This raises the prospect that states or other terrorists may piggyback on a conflict in unpredictable ways, and that future opponents may see a counterterrorism campaign or asymmetric war not as a deterrent but as a window of opportunity in terms of U.S. vulnerability and confusion.

This raises major new questions about the future of arms control and the value of existing arms control agreements. It also raises questions about the ability of states and terrorist groups to conduct anonymous attacks with highly lethal or costly CBRN weapons, particularly those of the biological variety. This not only raises the specter that one lesson of Afghanistan is that future opponents should use smallpox or its equivalent; it also raises the specter of how the United States would deal with anonymous attacks on its economy equivalent to the hoof-and-mouth outbreak in Britain or the swine fever outbreak in Taiwan.

Finally, it raises many of the same questions that Iraqi CBRN facilities and weapons did during the Gulf War. The United States has been developing sensors and targeting aids designed to "look" inside suspect buildings and facilities for well over a decade. It is unclear whether any such UAVs and unattended sensors are operational or that they are effective. UAVs can cover traffic going in and out of fixed and hardened facilities but not traffic inside them. CBRN weapons and activities can be dispersed into relatively small facilities, as can many delivery systems and munitions. In many cases it is impossible to distinguish between CBRN weapons and facilities and other military weapons and facilities, and it is equally difficult to distinguish CBRN weapons and facilities from civilian weapons and facilities.

The physical destruction of CBRN weapons and facilities also presents problems even when they can be targeted. Instead of minimizing collateral damage around the immediate target, it is crucial to limit any risk that such attacks will disseminate CBRN agents. The United States is examining weapons with suitable burning effects as well as less destructive means such as hardened sealing foams. CBRN kill does, however, remain a problem and would have raised serious issues if it had been known that Al Qaeda possessed CBRN weapons.

HARD-TARGET KILL CAPABILITY

Afghanistan had only a few classic shelters and hard targets left over from the days of the Soviet occupation and none had serious military meaning. It did, however, have many caves and a number were improved by Al Qaeda to become highly survivable and well-concealed targets. The United States used a wide range of ISR systems to try to find and characterize such caves and shelters, and it did find many. It could virtually never fully characterize the nature of the target any more than it could "look inside" ordinary buildings and surface facilities. Many were found only by troops on the ground and that could penetrate into the caves, and many may never have been discovered or assigned the correct priority.[51]

During the fighting, the United States placed a great deal of public emphasis on its use of specially configured bombs and weapons to attack caves and other hardened targets. These weapons included the use of the 15,000-pound "Daisy Cutter" against a mountain face with a number of caves.[52]

These weapons also included the GBU-28 "bunker buster," a 5,000-pound bomb originally developed during the Gulf War to kill hard targets like the shelters used by Saddam Hussein. This weapon uses a GPS or laser guidance system and can use software to produce a deep dive to increase its penetrating capability; it also uses a new cap with an elongated spike made out of nickel-cobalt steel alloy that can double the penetration of the weapon against some buried surfaces. Other such weapons include the GBU-15, GBU-24, and GBU-27. They included the AGM-130 rocket-propelled bomb—a 2,900-pound weapon with a similar warhead and with both GPS and video camera guidance—that F-15Es can fire 40 miles from the target.[53]

The most striking such weapon was a new form of fuel-air explosive (FAE), the BLU-118/B thermobaric munition, which was dropped on Al-Qaeda and Taliban targets near Gardez on March 2, 2002, the same day the USAF flew its first A-10 sorties in close air support missions out of bases in Pakistan. Like earlier FAE weapons, the BLU-118/B uses a fuel-rich chemical mixture to combat, rather than detonate, in a way that produces a long-duration, high-temperature pulse that creates an extremely high overpressure that can kill people (10 pounds per square inch) and damage vehicles (50 pounds per square inch). It uses the same penetrating warhead as the BLU-109 2,000-pound bomb and can be used on GBU-15 glide bombs, GBU-24 laser-guided bombs, and AGM-130 air-to-ground missiles.[54] The BLU-118/B is a first-generation weapon, however, and much more sophisticated forms of this weapon are under development for hard-target kills.[55]

U.S. Special Forces may also have made use of an experimental special cannon called the "Deep Digger," designed to eat into caves and bunkers by using a rapid series of explosions and secondary explosions. The USAF prepared 50 AGM-86D cruise missiles with hard-target kill warheads but may not have used them.[56]

Because of targeting reasons or because the effects were not serious enough, it is unclear whether most of these strikes produced any meaningful battle damage. In at least some cases, the United States seems to have fired such weapons against caves to inhibit their use, and it struck at cave entrances more to intimidate those inside than try to actually damage or kill the target. It is unclear whether any such attacks had any real success in terms of major damage. What is clear, however, is that it was often difficult to even target and launch against entrances when overhangs were present or terrain was shielding the target.

In short, the United States may be developing effective intelligence, targeting, and kill capabilities. But it did little more in Afghanistan than bang away—with unknown psychological and deterrent effects—at hardened targets.

CONFLICT TERMINATION, NATION BUILDING, GRAND STRATEGY, AND THE AFTERMATH OF MILITARY VICTORY

Victory is rarely total and is usually ambiguous. It has already become clear, however, that it may be much harder to win the peace than the actual war, particularly in terms of Afghan nation building and ensuring that some Taliban-like movement does not arise in the future. By mid-2002 there were serious clashes between warlords, at least one major assassination, and cases of Afghan factions trying to use the U.S. and British military to achieve their own tactical and political ends.

Neighboring powers, like Iran and Pakistan, started to play the Afghan Great Game even before the fall of Kabul, and any effort to create even a federal or cantonal Afghan state faces major political, ethnic, and economic challenges. The Gulf War, Lebanon, Somalia, Kosovo, and Bosnia have shown that even the most impressive tactical or strategic military victory can lose much or all of its meaning if it is followed by a diplomatic and political power vacuum or failure to achieve grand strategic goals.[57]

It is also unclear in mid-2002 whether the United States will really attempt to come to grips with this aspect of the war. It is very clear that the Department of Defense does not want to keep U.S. forces engaged or provide massive support to an allied peacemaking force. The preferred goal seems to be to try to create an Afghan national army and police force. On this front, however, the United States faces numerous challenges.

The United States and other coalition partners have set a goal of establishing a 60,000-person Afghan National Army (ANA) that will have the skills, weaponry, and discipline necessary to assist in maintaining peace and stability within Afghanistan. In May 2002 coalition nations met in Geneva to discuss funding the new army and concluded that roughly $290 million would need to be spent to cover the costs of creating and maintaining the new force. At that same meeting, the United States agreed to pay $70 million of the total cost. The Afghan Ministry of Defense agreed to provide weapons and assist in the recruitment of men from Afghanistan's 32 ethnically diverse provinces.[58]

On May 14, a small group of U.S. Army (USA) Special Forces began to train the first battalion of what will eventually be an 18-battalion force. At the same time, French troops began training a second battalion. The lack of a basic communications infrastructure in Afghanistan has hampered efforts to recruit enough soldiers and start training on time. Often only two-thirds of a battalion will be present at the start of the ten-week program of instruction (POI). Additional recruits arrive throughout the first few weeks of the POI, causing problems for instructors who cannot continually extend the training period and train those recruits who missed the initial weeks. While the USA has organized airlifts to transport recruits from more remote locations to the training center outside of Kabul, starting and completing training on time remains a long-term challenge.[59]

Outside nations cannot put an end to the problems caused by Afghanistan's warlords and tribal and ethnic divisions. They cannot constantly compensate for actions like the inability of the Afghan Defense Ministry to follow through on its pledge to provide weapons, which has led to a shortage of Kalashnikov-series assault rifles, medium machine guns, rocket-propelled grenade launchers, recoilless rifles, and mortars. To help alleviate the equipment shortage, Romania has donated 1,000 AK-37s and more than 200,000 rounds of 7.62mm ammunition, Turkey has provided uniforms, Italy has supplied antiriot gear, and Germany has provided vehicles.[60]

Outside nations, however, cannot help resolve the shortage of recruits, and unless regional warlords agree to relinquish control of their troops and arms, there may be only limited success in creating a multiethnic, national army. The United States had initially hoped that each of Afghanistan's 32 provinces would provide 20 men per battalion, thus ensuring an ethnically mixed force. Several provinces, however, have been unable to supply such manpower.[61]

Although efforts have been made to publicize the amount of pay that enlisted members in the new army will receive—recruits receive $30 per month while in training, and upon completion of the POI they see their salaries increase to $50 per month—recruits often arrive at training under the impression that their pay will be much higher. Many of these same recruits leave the training program within the first two weeks, leading to a battalion size of roughly 400 men by the end of only the second week of the POI. Long-term retention is also problematic. Of 550 soldiers trained by the British during a six-week program in April, roughly one-third have since deserted. As of late June 2002, the ANA's first battalion, which was nearing completion of the POI, consisted of only 380 soldiers.[62]

During training, U.S. and other coalition instructors must overcome language barriers as well as the educational background of the Afghan recruits, 70 percent of whom are illiterate. Language specialists must translate all orders into Farsi or Pashto and, in some cases, less-known Afghan dialects. Although recruits are continually assigned to multiethnic teams and encouraged to allow their competitive instincts to be directed toward defeating other teams rather than each other, ethnic divisions remain a stumbling block to the successful formation of the ANA. Further compounding problems of the growth of the ANA is the unclear status of 18,000 former United Front mujahideen fighters under the command of the Afghan defense minister, Muhammad Fahim Khan, who are currently being "reorganized." Some observers feel that Fahim opposes the development of a multiethnic Afghan army because such a force would undermine the level of power and influence that ethnic Tajiks, who comprised much of the Northern Alliance, currently hold in Afghanistan's armed forces.[63]

One of the key problems is the Western tendency to try to accomplish in weeks or months key activities that require years of patient and consistent effort. Military officials agree that 10 weeks is not nearly enough time for troops to develop the skills necessary for effective performance in an environment like Afghanistan. The lack of previous experience and the shortened training period are further affected by the lack of a preexisting corps of noncommissioned officers. U.S. commanders are working toward a resolution of this problem. In an attempt to address longer-term training deficiencies, the United States plans to organize additional follow-on training courses that will allow the new army to refine and develop much needed real-world skills. French troops who are responsible for training the second through the fifth battalions of the ANA indicate that it will take between one and two years for the initial five battalions to become the strong nucleus of the new army. However, before additional training courses can be initiated, long-term equipment and funding problems must be resolved.[64]

It is almost certain the Afghan government will remain dependent for years on Western aid to alleviate both of these problems, and even then the failure to deal with Afghanistan's warlord problem immediately after the fall of Kabul and deploy peacekeepers nationwide will create a wide range of problems. In the absence of an income tax, the Afghan finance minister, Ashraf Ghani, estimates that even if warlords begin paying the customs taxes that they owe the new government, only $80 million of the roughly $460 million total Afghan budget will be funded. Western nations will likely be called on to assist in the elimination of this revenue shortfall.[65]

While U.S. military officials are cautiously optimistic that the security situation in Afghanistan will remain stable enough to allow new battalions of the ANA to receive additional training and develop additional confidence and discipline, the security situation could easily worsen and threaten the survival and long-term prospects for the ANA. In addition, the immediate mission and role of ANA battalions, once out of training, remains unclear. Given the challenges that must be overcome before the ANA can be considered an effective security force, a continued U.S. and coalition military presence in Afghanistan will be a key element of any postconflict strategy.[66]

Additional military and security obstacles to a successful nation-building attempt in Afghanistan include the continued hostilities among ethnic groups and continued fighting among warlords. U.S. officials are increasingly concerned that Al Qaeda leaders may be holding discussions with several rogue warlords, including Gulbuddin Hekmatyar, an influential Pashtun who still commands a small group of 1,000–2,000 troops and has access to money that could be of assistance to any Al Qaeda attempt to reorganize. The CIA considered Hekmatyar to be such a serious threat to peace and stability in Afghanistan that it unsuccessfully attempted to assassinate him by firing a missile from a Predator drone at what was thought to be his location.[67]

Reemerging ethnic tension reinforces the problems created by a weak central government, warlords, factionalism, ethnic division in the government, uncertain and insufficient economic aid, and Western efforts to rush the job or leave it. Following the July 1, 2002, incident in Oruzgan province (see page 40) in which a U.S. AC-130 gunship accidentally fired on a wedding party in the village of Kakarak, killing and injuring several civilians, Kandahar governor Gul Agha Shirzai met with the governor of Oruzgan and several provinces dominated by ethnic Pashtuns. The meeting resulted in an announcement by Shirzai that the governors of the region would require the United States to contact them for permission before initiating military actions in any of the Pashtun provinces. More significantly, however, the meeting also resulted in the creation of two new, armed militias that will be overseen not by the central government but by the regional governors. Although one of the militias is designated to work along with U.S. and coalition forces in hunting for rogue fighters, U.S. officials view the action of the governors as undermining coalition attempts to create a national army. In the event of future instability, the regional governors could use the new militias as their own security force, similar to the way in which Afghan warlords used their own militias during the internal ethnic fighting that engulfed the nation for a decade.[68]

At the same time, the events of July 1 may cause the Bush administration and CENTCOM to reevaluate their initial view of the role that U.S. military forces should play in Afghanistan. Following the July 1 incident, the commander of U.S. forces in Afghanistan, Lt. Gen. Dan McNeil, assigned civil affairs officers and humanitarian workers to the areas affected by the U.S. military action. These civil affairs officers are to work closely with Afghan villagers and other U.S. forces in rebuilding infrastructure devastated during the years of war. Projects include the construction of wells, schools, and a power plant. Beyond these tasks, however, the goal of these forces is to win over the "heart and minds" of the native Pashtun population that, following the accidental U.S. attack, has expressed anger at continued U.S. military operations in Oruzgan province, long a haven of Taliban and Al Qaeda militants.[69]

Coalitions based on only the principle that the "enemy of my enemy is my friend" are clearly proving inadequate for both nation building and war fighting. As the fighting in Afghanistan continues, however, U.S. civilian and military leaders are examining the necessity of adapting the force mix in Afghanistan. With most remaining Al Qaeda and Taliban fighters operating in small groups along the border with Pakistan, these U.S. officials argue that the next step in ensuring Afghanistan's future stability depends on the U.S. military's ability to build a trusting relationship between itself and the ethnic tribes that make up the Afghan population. Such a mission would involve the participation of greater numbers of civil affairs officers than are currently stationed in Afghanistan and would entail expanding a current program under which the United States maintains military contacts with several Afghan villages.

Civil affairs battalions are in short supply, however, as are other branches of the Special Forces, and there is a shortage of sergeants to man future Special Forces teams. CENTCOM is also evaluating dispatching USA military police to Afghanistan to serve as a quick-action protective team for U.S. forces currently located throughout the country. Regardless of any personnel shortages, the fact that the United States is reevaluating the role that the military will play in rebuilding Afghanistan signifies a realization on the part of the Bush administration that the problems that Afghanistan faces go far beyond the threat of remaining Al Qaeda fighters.[70]

The central fact remains that grand strategy always requires more than military victory. Conflict termination cannot always end in successful nation building. Transforming cultures, political systems, and economies is far harder than most advocates of nation building would like to admit; and it is often impossible or too costly to attempt, much less sustain, until it is truly successful. Nevertheless, victory is only victory when the use of force is tied to the best achievable political and economic outcome and level of postconflict stability.[71]

Even if the Afghan problem is solved, it still cannot be a true strategic victory in grand strategic terms. If the United States must mix force with diplomacy and allied support in some 68 countries, it must have a broader definition of victory and be able to communicate both that definition and its progress toward meeting it. As of mid-2002, U.S. efforts at this are episodic at best, and the overall grand strategy and conflict termination aspects of the U.S. battle against Al Qaeda are as unclear as its goals regarding the defeat of global terrorism.

There is a curious irony in the fact that the U.S. government and Department of Defense seem to have been only marginally more concerned with planning for conflict termination and grand strategic outcomes in Afghanistan than they were during the Gulf War and the war in Kosovo. This failure to give conflict termination the same priority as military operations, and grand strategy the same priority as strategy, is particularly striking because many senior officials in the present Bush administration have been deeply involved in trying to come to grips with the result of a similar failure in the Gulf War and the survival of Saddam Hussein.

There is a similar irony in the fact that the Bush administration's criticism of the Clinton administration's vacuous moral posturing and hopeless optimism and false promises surrounding the Dayton Accords and conflict aftermath in Kosovo has tended to be replaced by an equally vacuous effort to avoid being deeply involved in the aftermath of Afghanistan.

Afghanistan is yet another blunt warning that it is time that U.S. war planners begin to plan for true victory, not simply defeat of enemy military forces. The time—if it ever existed—when military planners needed to plan only for war is long over. In fact, it seems fair to say that war plans that do not include peace plans have always been signs of gross military incompetence.

It may be unpopular that most postconflict peace involves some form of prolonged occupation, peacekeeping, and nation building, but it is a fact that military action can have lasting benefits only if the military (and their political leaders) are willing to pay the necessary price. In war, more than in any other human activity, no country should begin what it is not prepared to finish, and few modern wars magically result in desirable governments, economies, societies, and patterns of alliance simply because the fighting ends. The officer who cannot adjust to this reality is unfit to wear a uniform. The political leader unwilling to face this reality is at best creating a recipe for military futility and at worst a recipe for disaster.

NOTES

[1] See *New York Times,* March 4, 2002, p. 1; *Washington Post,* February 10, 2002, p. A-1; March 4, 2002, p. A-1; May 8, 2002, p. A-16; *Christian Science Monitor,* March 4, 2002, p. 1.

[2] *Washington Post,* December 23, 2001, p. A-12; February 10, 2002, p. A-1; May 30, 2002, p. 1; June 18, 2002, p. A-12; *International Herald Tribune,* December 11, 2001, p.1; March 11, 2002, p. 3; *London Times,* March 4, 2002; *Christian Science Monitor,* March 4, 2002, p. 1.

[3] *New York Times,* February 4, 2002; March 27, 2002; May 1, 2002; May 3, 2002; May 6, 2002, p. 1; June 3, 2002; *London Times,* March 4, 2002; *Washington Post,* December 23, 2001, p. A-10; March 20, 2002, p.A-1; May 14, 2002, p. A-15; May 16, 2002, p. A-1; June 27, 2002, pp. A-1 and A-28; *Washington Times,* May 15, 2002, p. 3; May 29, 2002, p. 4; June 24, 2002, p. 15; June 27, 2002, p.16; June 28, 2002, p. 1; June 29, 2002; *Newsweek,* June 10, 2002; *USA Today,* June 13, 2002, p. 1; June 18, 2002, p. 7; *Los Angeles Times,* May 1, 2002; May 14, 2002; June 11, 2002, p. 1; June 28, 2002; *Chicago Tribune,* May 30, 2002; June 23, 2002; June 30, 2002; *Christian Science Monitor,* March 22, 2002, p.1; June 27, 2002; June 28, 2002, p. 1; July 2, 2002, p. 1; *Insight,* July 22, 2002; *Time,* July 1, 2002, p. 26; *London Daily Telegraph,* March 21, 2002; June 24, 2002; *Wall Street Journal,* December 12, 2001; *Jane's Defense Weekly,* October 17, 2001, p. 21; October 31, 2001, p. 3; John G. Roos, "Turning Up the Heat," *Armed Forces Journal,* February 2002, pp. 36–42.

[4] *Philadelphia Inquirer,* June 26, 2002.

[5] For example, see the warning of Secretary of Defense Donald Rumsfeld on June 3, 2002. *Washington Post,* June 4, 2002, p. A-1.

[6] *Sunday Telegraph,* January 13, 2002, p. 17.

[7] *Washington Times,* June 21, 2002, p. A-1.

⁸ For a short unclassified overview, see "What's become of Al-Qaeda," *Time,* January 21, 2002, pp. 18–22.

⁹ *USA Today,* June 25, 2002, p. 18.

¹⁰ Ibid.; *New York Times,* July 3, 2002.

¹¹ *New York Times,* July 3, 2002.

¹² See Anthony H. Cordesman, *The Lessons and Non-Lessons of the Air and Missile Campaign in Kosovo* (Westport, Conn.: Praeger, 2001).

¹³ Office of the Secretary of Defense, *Annual Report on the Military Power of the People's Republic of China, Report to Congress Pursuant to the FY2000 National Defense Authorization Act* (Washington, D.C.: Department of Defense, July 2002), pp. 11–14, www.dod.gov/news/Jul2002/d20020712china.pdf.

¹⁴ *Washington Post,* July 4, 2002, p. 16.

¹⁵ *New York Times,* July 14, 2002, p. A-1.

¹⁶ *Washington Post,* July 4, 2002, p. 16; *New York Times,* July 14, 2002, p. A-1; *Boston Globe,* July 4, 2002, p. 1.

¹⁷ *New York Times,* February 8, 2002, p. A-14.

¹⁸ *Washington Post,* February 7, 2002, p. A-12; February 20, 2002, pp. A-1, A-8, A-9.

¹⁹ *New York Times,* July 7, 2002, p. 8.

²⁰ See Laura Kind, "A Civilian Toll in Afghan War Likely Lower," *Philadelphia Inquirer,* February 12, 2002, p. 1. The Associated Press estimate of civilian deaths includes 70 in Kabul, 81 in Kandahar, 55 in Jalalabad, 10 in Mazar-i-Sharif, 18 in Herat, 25 around Spin Boldak, 55 in Karam, and 167 in the Tora Bora region (155 in Kama, 5 in Agom, and 7 in Pacair). Also see Barry Bearak, "Uncertain Toll in the Fog of War," *New York Times,* February 10, 2002, p. A-1.

²¹ For a detailed description of the real-world problems encountered on the ground, see Dana Priest, "In War, Mud Huts and Hard Calls," *Washington Post,* February 20, 2002, pp. A-1 and A-8.

²² *New York Times,* July 21, 2002, p. 1.

²³ Ibid.

²⁴ *Washington Post,* February 7, 2002, p. A-12; *Washington Post,* February 20, 2002, pp. A-1 and A-8; *New York Times,* February 8, 2002, p. A-14; *Philadelphia Inquirer,* February 12, 2002, p. 1; for Gen. Tommy Franks's testimony to the Senate Armed Services Committee on February 7, 2002, see www.senate.gov/~armed_services/statemnt/2002/Franks.pdf.

[25] *Washington Post,* February 22, 2002, p. A-18.

[26] *New York Times,* February 12, 2002, p. A-7.

[27] *New York Times,* July 7, 2002, p. 8.

[28] *Time,* July 15, 2002, p. 32; *Washington Post,* July 2, 2002, A-1; Associated Press, July 2, 2002; *Washington Post,* July 9, 2002, p. 17.

[29] *New York Times,* July 7, 2002, p. 8.; *Time,* July 15, 2002, p. 32; *Washington Post,* July 9, 2002, p. 17.

[30] *Washington Post,* July 9, 2002, p. 17; *New York Times,* July 4, 2002, p. 6; July 7, 2002; *Washington Times,* July 12, 2002, p. 10.

[31] *The Guardian,* July 2, 2002.

[32] *New York Times,* July 7, 2002, p. 8.

[33] *New York Times* (from wire reports), July 2, 2002.

[34] Associated Press, July 2, 2002.

[35] *London Daily Telegraph,* July 5, 2002.

[36] *New York Times,* July 14, 2002.

[37] *Washington Post,* July 9, 2002, p. 17.

[38] Ibid.; *Washington Times,* July 9, 2002, p. 1.

[39] *New York Times,* July 21, 2002, p. 1.

[40] The counts of total weapons used at given periods are approximate. General Franks referred to 18,000 in his testimony to the Senate Armed Services on February 7, 2002, www.senate.gov/~armed_services/statemnt/2002/Franks.pdf.

[41] See Human Rights Watch and the Project for Defense Alternatives for some of the better estimates. Also see Chip Cummins, "Military Avoids Estimate of Civilian Deaths," *Wall Street Journal,* December 4, 2002; Barry Bearak, "Uncertain Toll in the Fog of War"; Laura King, "Civilian Death Toll in Afghan War Likely Lower," *Philadelphia Inquirer,* February 12, 2002, p. 1; David Zucchino, *Times* (London), June 2, 2002, p. 1; William M. Arkin, "Checking on Civilian Casualties," April 9, 2002, www.washingtonpost.com/wp-dyn/nation/columns/dotmil/; and *The Estimate* 14, no. 1, January 11, 2002, www.theestimate.com.

[42] James G. Roche, "Transforming the Air Force," *Joint Forces Quarterly,* Autumn/Winter 2001–2002, pp. 9–12; Sweetman, "The Falling Price of Precision."

[43] Sweetman, "The Falling Price of Precision."

[44] *Aerospace Daily,* December 5, 2001.

[45] *Chicago Tribune,* February 6, 2002.

⁴⁶ *Dallas Morning News,* May 31, 2002.

⁴⁷ *Los Angeles Times,* January 21, 2002, p. A-1.

⁴⁸ Ibid.; *Chicago Tribune,* February 6, 2002.

⁴⁹ W. Hays Parks, "Air War and the Law of War," *Air Force Law Review* 32 (1990), p. 1.

⁵⁰ For typical reporting on Al Qaeda activity see: *Washington Post,* March 12, 2002, p. 1; *Washington Times,* April 11, 2002, p. 1; Associated Press, February 1, 2002; *Time,* June 24, 2002, p. 24; Reuters, December 12, 2002; *New York Times,* February 26, 2002, p. 1; March 20, 2002; March 23, 2002, p. 1; *USA Today,* March 26, 2002, p. 10.

⁵¹ For discussion of U.S. wartime technology developments see *Los Angeles Times,* March 17, 2002, p. 1; *Washington Post,* March 26, 2002, p. 16.

⁵² *New York Times,* December 11, 2002, p. 1; *Jane's Defense Weekly,* March 13, 2002, p. 6.

⁵³ *Washington Post,* December 13, 2001, p. 22; *Jane's Defense Weekly,* May 2, 2001, pp. 24–27.

⁵⁴ *Jane's Defense Weekly,* March 13, 2002, p. 6.

⁵⁵ *Jane's International Defense Review,* April 2002, p. 3.

⁵⁶ *New York Times,* December 3, 2001; *Jane's Defense Weekly,* May 2, 2001, pp. 24–27.

⁵⁷ Good early summaries of this problem appeared in "Afghanistan's Interim Government: Strengths and Weaknesses," *The Estimate,* December 14, 2001, www.theestimate.com. For typical reporting on the problems involved, see *New York Times,* February 21, 2002, p. 1; June 6, 2002; July 11, 2002; July 23, 2002; *The Estimate,* June 26, 2002, www.theestimate.com; *Washington Post,* February 21, 2002, p. 15; July 8, 2002, p. 13; July 9, 2002, p. 1; *Economist,* June 8, 2002, pp. 22–24; June 22, 2002, p. 39; July 13, 2002, p. 35; *Los Angeles Times,* February 25, 2002, p. 1; *Boston Globe,* June 24, 2002, p. 1; *USA Today,* June 28, 2002, p. 17.

⁵⁸ *Boston Globe,* June 24, 2002, A-1; *Wall Street Journal,* June 27, 2002.

⁵⁹ *Jane's Defense Weekly,* June 12–19, 2002, pp. 26–27; *Boston Globe,* June 24, 2002, p. A-1.

⁶⁰ Ibid., *Wall Street Journal,* June 27, 2002.

⁶¹ *Wall Street Journal,* June 27, 2002.

⁶² *Jane's Defense Weekly,* June 12–19, 2002, pp. 26–27; *Wall Street Journal,* June 27, 2002.

⁶³ Ibid.

[64] Ibid.

[65] *Wall Street Journal,* June 27, 2002.

[66] *Jane's Defense Weekly,* June 12–19, 2002, pp. 26–27.

[67] *Boston Globe,* July 4, 2002, p. A-1.

[68] See article by Alissa J. Rubin, *Los Angeles Times,* July 15, 2002.

[69] *Washington Times,* July 15, 2002, p. A-1; *Los Angeles Times,* July 15, 2002.

[70] *Washington Times,* July 15, 2002, p. A-1.

[71] For a very good in-depth discussion of these issues, see John R. Boule II, "Operational Planning and Conflict Termination," *Joint Forces Quarterly,* Autumn/Winter 2001–2002, pp. 97–102.

CHAPTER FIVE

POWER PROJECTION AND
FORCE TRANSFORMATION

Remembering it is dangerous to generalize without more detailed data on the forces engaged in the Afghan conflict and the history of their battles and engagements and also remembering it is dangerous to generalize at all given the unique character of the Afghan conflict, some lessons about force transformation and power projection do seem clear.

The Afghan War has demonstrated once again the need to be able to project land and airpower rapidly over very long distances. It has demonstrated the value of strategic airlift and long-range strike capability and the value of being able to operate with limited forward basing. At the same time, it has confirmed the value of light forces, like Special Forces, in counterterrorism efforts and some forms of asymmetric warfare. The conflict in Afghanistan has also demonstrated that planning for major regional contingencies and wars where the United States must fight against heavy armor and heavily defended airspace is only one possible scenario in a changing spectrum of conflicts.

During the fighting in Afghanistan, the United States has relied heavily on strategic airlift capabilities to transport forces and equipment to the battlefield and forward-staging areas. The heavy reliance on airlift capabilities, however, has revealed several shortcomings in U.S. airlift capability. A USAF study anticipates an increase in the need for strategic airlift capabilities and calls for the purchase of 60 new C-17 cargo planes. The U.S. Air Force estimates that of 5,500 missions in Afghanistan, the C-17 was involved in 2,872. The USAF also claims that C-17s have transported roughly 44,000 personnel, 100,000 tons of cargo, 636 medical patients, and 565 Al Qaeda and Taliban detainees.[1]

The USMC fleet of roughly 50 KC-130s is aging and in need of serious maintenance and upgrades. As of January 2002, the majority of the KC-130s in Afghanistan were not equipped with night vision equipment and the advanced radar systems used in combat aircraft. Because the aircraft are vulnerable to attacks from shoulder-launched missiles—a popular weapon among Al Qaeda and Taliban fighters—they have been forced to fly only at night, making night navigation capabilities essential. A lack of night vision and terrain avoidance radar was cited by the U.S. Department of Defense as a major factor leading to a January 9 accident in which a KC-130 crashed into the side of a mountain in Afghanistan. The KC-130J, the next generation of the aircraft, is equipped with the necessary night navigation equipment. The lack of such equipment on current aircraft, however, suggests that the military must focus additional funding on improving operational effectiveness.[2]

Although Afghanistan did not stress the total pool of U.S. airlift assets, the conflict once again indicates how critical adequate total lift capacity can be in larger wars. Note that various war games show that the United States is 10–15 million ton miles short of a requirement for total strategic lift capacity of 54.5 million ton miles. The United States is now buying C-17s at the rate of one per month to fill this gap, and the C-17 showed in Afghanistan that its ability to use relatively unimproved airfields did have practical advantage. The United States has an inventory of approximately 120 C-17s and plans to buy 60–120 more. It is also replacing the engines and updating the avionics on its 23 aging C-5s and is seeking to buy 150 more C-130J tactical airlift aircraft.[3]

Even with these additions, U.S. airlift would still be under severe strain to support one major regional contingency through at least 2019, and the United States is the only NATO country with significant dedicated strategic airlift.[4] Britain has leased C-17s and plans to replace some of its 44 C-130s with A400Ms but has not yet bought a strategic-lift aircraft. France plans to buy such aircraft but the timing, scale, and capacity involved are still far from clear.[5]

GROUND OPERATIONS: LESSONS OF OPERATION ANACONDA

In March 2002, U.S. and friendly Afghan forces initiated the first large ground operation—Operation Anaconda—involving significant U.S. forces; the goal of the operation was to eliminate Al Qaeda forces that had been massing in a 60-square-mile portion of the Shah-i-Kot valley near the Afghanistan-Pakistan border. The terrain, which is characterized by steep mountains, presented an ideal environment for Al Qaeda fighters to operate for it provided them with significant cover as well as numerous options for escape.

Military planners were careful to learn from the lessons of Tora Bora. U.S. Special Forces trained Afghan forces how to advance successfully and seize territory while in battle and instructed them not to advance and retreat during battle as they had done in the past. Also, instead of relying heavily on Afghan forces to do most of the fighting as it had at Tora Bora, the United States committed a larger number of troops to the new operation. This number increased further when it became apparent during the operation that an increased number of U.S. forces would be required to ensure success.[6]

The Battle Plan Is Still the First Casualty of War

According to the battle plan, the Afghan troops, led by a group of U.S. Special Forces, were to advance across the valley and force the enemy fighters to abandon their positions and head for the valley's eastern ridge where they would be met by additional forces blocking their escape. Additional Afghan and U.S. forces were positioned on the valley's southern end, sealing off Al Qaeda escape routes in an attempt to block a repeat of the outcome at Tora Bora, when U.S. forces prevailed but a number of Al Qaeda and Taliban fighters escaped.[7]

During the development of the battle plan for Anaconda, senior defense officials spent several weeks analyzing data gathered from ISR missions in the region. As events unfolded, however, a number of intelligence shortcomings became apparent: source limitations in present ISR assets, ability to detect infiltration and concentration of light infantry forces, ability to "kill" hard targets like caves, and the ability to detect and interdict the exfiltration and dispersal of infantry. Mission planners did not have a clear idea of how many Al Qaeda and Taliban fighters were in the valley. As the fighting progressed, initial estimates of "several hundred" fighters were later increased to roughly 1,000.[8] In addition to underestimating the size of the enemy force, mission planners were also unaware of the fighters' exact locations and unsure about whether the dispersed nature of the fighters was planned or the result of natural movements among forces.[9] Specifically, ISR data had failed to reflect the presence of several enemy fighters in well-fortified positions on the eastern ridge of the valley where U.S. forces were to be deployed.[10]

This shortcoming of U.S. ISR capabilities contributed to an unanticipated series of events on the third day of the operation. During the early morning hours of March 4, a U.S. MH-47 Chinook helicopter carrying U.S. Special Forces, Navy SEAL special operations forces, and a USAF special operations combat controller touched down atop Takur Ghar mountain. U.S. aircraft had previously bombed the ridge, located at an altitude of 10,200 feet, and surveillance missions conducted after these bombing runs had not revealed any hidden enemy positions. When preparing to disembark the helicopter, however, the U.S. special operations forces were met with heavy enemy fire. In the confusion that followed, the helicopter, despite its now damaged electrical and hydraulic system, began a shaky lift off that caused one of the SEALS to fall down the cargo ramp and out of the aircraft. Under continuing fire, the helicopter was forced to leave the crew member there, and it touched down a number of miles away.[11]

In the immediate aftermath, a rescue effort to retrieve the lost crew member was launched. During that mission, some aspects of *Black Hawk Down* repeated themselves. Several Apache helicopters were disabled; and another Chinook helicopter carrying an Army Ranger extraction force was brought down by enemy fire, immediately killing four crew soldiers. A second group of Army Rangers—

burdened with heavy equipment, extra layers of clothing, and inappropriate footwear—was forced to ascend the mountain where it met the surviving Rangers and assaulted enemy positions while waiting several hours to be extracted with the wounded and dead. In all, seven soldiers died in the incident and roughly another eleven were wounded, the highest number of combat deaths to occur in one day since eighteen U.S. Marines died in operations in Somalia.[12]

These and the other events that transpired during the initial day of Operation Anaconda provide several lessons. In addition to revealing continued shortcomings in U.S. ISR capabilities, they call into question the effectiveness of U.S. airpower in destroying well-entrenched enemy positions. Also the fighting on Takur Ghar further supports current conclusions regarding the difficulties of fighting in an unconventional environment against an opponent who is difficult to locate and target. Throughout the fighting on that day, and throughout the entire operation, U.S. commanders were forced to alter battle plans, and ground forces were forced to adapt constantly to a rapidly changing situation in which their equipment was either inappropriate or an impediment to their progress.

This battle also showed that airpower and allies are not always a substitute for U.S. ground troops. Anaconda represented the first time during the fighting in Afghanistan that the United States introduced significant numbers of ground troops into the battlefield. Roughly 2,000 coalition troops—including 500 U.S. regular troops from mountain and airborne divisions, 450 Special Forces, and 200 specially trained troops from Australia, Canada, Denmark, France, Germany, and Norway—participated in the fighting, in addition to a significant number of Afghan forces. The start of the operations was delayed 48 hours owing to poor weather conditions in the region that, while characteristic of the Afghan winter, were not conducive to launching a military operation in mountainous terrain. Weather remained a constraining factor throughout the operation, at times limiting the ability of the United States to provide air support for ongoing ground operations. When the operation finally began, the original plans quickly fell apart.[13]

Afghan forces were quickly ambushed by Al Qaeda and Taliban fighters when they entered the valley, and they awaited instructions from the Special Forces team accompanying them; this forced them to withdraw. U.S. commanders responded by inserting, via CH-47 and MH-47 Chinook helicopters, several hundred U.S. Army soldiers.[14] Upon landing, however, these forces came under direct fire from fighters pre-positioned in defensive positions and equipped with small arms, rocket launchers, and shoulder-fired surface-to-air missiles.[15] U.S. commanders later admitted that the number of Al Qaeda entrenched in the area, as well as the intensity with which they had fought, had surprised them.[16]

Throughout the early stages of the operation, U.S. planners appear to have underestimated the size and strength of the enemy force they would be facing. This, in part, can be attributed to their reliance on a small group of local Afghan commanders and informants who may have painted an inaccurate picture of the enemy.[17] Even the most advanced ISR technology has its limitations, however, which underscores the importance of developing accurate human intelligence.

UAVs and other sensor platforms, although they provide detailed imagery of the battlefield, cannot "see" through mountains and under heavy brush to reveal well-hidden enemy positions. U.S. tactical communications often lacked line of sight and either failed or saturated local satellite communications capabilities. By choosing the mountainous valley as the battlefield, Al Qaeda was able to maximize its asymmetric advantage. If the United States is to be successful against dispersed forces in the future, it must develop means of more precisely determining the location of enemy forces in order to avoid accidentally sending soldiers into heavily entrenched enemy positions, as happened during the initial days of Operation Anaconda.[18]

Other lessons emerged during the first day of the battle, when helicopter-based firing power was not extremely effective in hitting enemy positions. Five AH-64 Apache gunships were called in to suppress enemy gunfire, but several quickly became damaged and were forced to withdraw. Although additional helicopters, including the USMC Super Cobra, were deployed to provide support and cover for ground forces, they did not operate at optimal levels owing to the extreme elevations at which the battle was occurring. Limited loiter time and the inability of the helicopters to hover in position negatively affected their targeting ability and decreased their accuracy.[19]

After 18 hours of fighting, in which one U.S. soldier and three Afghan soldiers were killed and another 40 U.S. soldiers were injured, the contingent of U.S. forces, along with the remaining Afghan forces, withdrew to a point near the town of Gardez.[20] After evaluating the failure of U.S. ground forces to be successful at forcing the Al Qaeda fighters toward the ridge and, during the initial hours of battle, at sealing off potential escape routes, commanders reverted to the pattern of heavy bombing used at Tora Bora.

The next phase of Operation Anaconda was largely air based, with B-52 heavy bombers dropping 200- and 500-pound bombs on Al Qaeda targets in the valley and along the mountains. The United States also successfully used two new 2,000-pound thermobaric bombs that, when fired into a cave, expel the oxygen and suffocate any hidden fighters. Following this stage of the battle, U.S. ground forces were able to operate effectively and, during the following two weeks, located and destroyed enemy positions in the valley.[21]

Although the use of airpower during Operation Anaconda was essential, some observers argue that the need for such intense air support revealed serious shortcomings in the capabilities of light ground forces. A recent report analyzing the U.S. Army's performance in Afghanistan cites a lack of artillery as a major shortcoming of the operations in Afghanistan. During Operation Anaconda, ground forces did not have the option of using artillery to target and destroy entrenched enemy positions. Army troops had to rely on their own mortars as well as air support from AH-64 Apache helicopters and combat aircraft to eliminate the enemy threat. In many cases, a direct hit from a 200-pound bomb was necessary to take out an enemy position.[22] In addition, further adaptations had to be made to the Apache helicopters.[23] Originally designed to attack Soviet armor at night, the helicopters' weapons systems were extensively modified before the Gulf War and were modified again in Kosovo. In Afghanistan, the helicopters were sporadically armed to increase their effectiveness at hitting entrenched ground forces. The high altitude of the operation, however, forced Apache helicopter pilots to engage in maneuvers that decreased their ability to target ground positions accurately. Unlike aircraft flying at higher altitudes, the Apaches were easily targeted and hit by small-arms fire and rocket-propelled grenades from Al Qaeda and Taliban fighters. Nevertheless, the Apache helicopters were more effective at destroying enemy positions than were fixed-winged aircraft. Following Operation Anaconda, A-10 aircraft were dispatched to the region to further support Apache operations.[24]

The Artillery-versus-Airpower Debate

In situations such as Operation Anaconda, where specific coordinates of enemy positions are unknown, some Army observers concluded that artillery, including howitzers, would be more effective than airpower at hitting enemy positions. The use of artillery is contingent, however, on the Army's ability to maneuver its current overweight, bulky equipment to locations near the battlefield. Given the rugged terrain in and around the Shah-i-Kot valley, an important question is how successful the Army would have been in deploying artillery.

Army chief of staff, Gen. Eric Shinseki, testified before the Senate Armed Services Committee that he felt artillery such as the Crusader would have provided ground forces with necessary "suppressive fires" in significantly less time than it took for aircraft to respond. While it took twenty-five minutes for aircraft to provide support, Shinseki testified, it would take the Crusader roughly only three minutes to provide support to ground forces in a similar situation. Citing the fact that 28 of 36 casualties during the operation were due to indirect mortar fire, Shinseki said that artillery would have been the most effective method of support for ground forces.[25] While he was lobbying hard to keep the Crusader program from being canceled, artillery was shipped into the theater in July.

Gen. Tommy Franks, head of CENTCOM, disagreed with Shinseki's assessment. Franks stated that the notion of transporting and positioning a number of Crusader howitzers for use during Operation Anaconda was "mind boggling." Franks, testifying before the Senate Defense Appropriations Subcommittee, stated that several factors—including lift availability, the altitude at which the battle was occurring, and the munition trajectory characteristics of a weapon—must be considered when determining whether to deploy artillery. Based on these factors, Franks concluded that mortars were a more appropriate weapon for use during Operation Anaconda.[26]

At least one officer in the 101st Airborne Division's 3rd Brigade was ambiguous when he commented on the issue. He noted that lift and basing requirements prevented the unit from bringing its 18 M-109 155mm howitzers into the theater as well as some of its UH-60 helicopters. At the same time, this officer felt that light 105mm towed howitzers weighed only 4,400 pounds and moving them to the battlefield would not delay or complicate operations. He did note that artillery weapons have to be secured and require support and that 120mm mortars are more mobile. He also noted, however, that they have an effective range of 7,200 meters—about half that of the 105mm howitzer—and must be moved, supported, and resupplied much farther forward, often under much more difficult resupply and force protection conditions.[27] It is interesting that the 82nd Airborne Division did bring its artillery weapons to the theater when it replaced the 101st.

The debate between Shinseki and Franks represents the larger debate over the practical uses of artillery in nonconventional settings. While having the Crusader or another howitzer present during Operation Anaconda would have been of assistance to ground forces, it is unlikely that the Army would have been able to transport it there. Even in ideal weather conditions—and the initial days of Operation Anaconda saw some of the worst winter weather in the mountains that Afghanistan offers—it would have taken several days to transport such heavy equipment to such a high altitude. If one of the lessons of Operation Anaconda is the need for artillery support even in rugged battle environments, then a complementary lesson is the need for lighter, more agile equipment to make the use of such artillery possible. Indeed, the demands placed on the Army during Operation Anaconda provide additional evidence in support of the Army transformation effort already under way.[28]

Equally important, in the real world hard trade-offs have to be made for resource reasons. The Crusader was designed at a time when unguided artillery rounds dominated artillery fire. The United States has at least five guided 155mm artillery shells under development and some—such as Excalibur and the trajectory correctable munition—have ranges in excess of 30 miles.[29] It is far too soon to know whether a combination of light artillery weapons, tactical ISR assets, and guided artillery rounds can provide a far more cost-effective solution than traditional upgrades to heavy artillery platforms. It also seems imprudent to rush into the procurement of extremely costly and heavy legacy systems.

The Weightlifting Contest

Under the current Army transformation plans, some of the equipment problems that U.S. troops have encountered in Afghanistan may be resolved as early as 2008. The Army is currently developing the Objective Force Warrior (OFW) with the goal of decreasing by half the weight of the equipment that soldiers carry.

During Operation Anaconda, ground forces often became overburdened by the weight and amount of weaponry they were carrying. Soldiers reported that in order to move more quickly they were forced to discard some of their equipment. In one instance, several Special Forces troops scaling the side of a mountain were forced to discard their body armor because it significantly inhibited their ability to ascend the steep mountainside.

On the basis of these common experiences and difficulties, it will be essential for the Army to reexamine basic equipment and weapons characteristics. Ground forces in fighting situations like Anaconda face several challenges and require the effective means to defend themselves and attack the enemy. Their equipment should not become an impediment to their survival or to advancing the main objectives of the mission.

As part of the development of the OFW, weapons made out of ultralight materials would replace the M-16A2 rifle, M-4 carbine, and M-249 squad automatic weapon. The new generation of weapons, although possessing similar capabilities, is being designed to weigh roughly 35 percent less than the current set of weapons. Also being developed as part of the OFW are alternative-energy technologies such as lightweight fuel cells that will power high-tech sensors and replace heavy batteries that currently weigh down soldiers. The new sensors will monitor the battlefield environment as well as the physical health of the troops in the field, allowing medics outside the battlefield to provide advice regarding troop readiness and injuries. A final component of the new uniform is the development of a camouflage technology that can adapt to the environment in which the troops are operating and maximize their concealment.[30]

A major additional component of the OFW program is the development of a robotic all-terrain vehicle (ATV) that will follow troops and carry roughly 500 pounds of equipment. This may be practical in a more traditional battlefield setting, but it is questionable whether such a vehicle would be of use to ground forces engaging an enemy in mountainous terrain that is difficult for humans, let alone robotic vehicles, to manage.[31]

Like many elements of the Army's future objective force, the OFW program is highly dependent on the development of other new technologies, including a uniform equipped with a microclimate conditioning system that will allow soldiers to operate comfortably in both hot and cold environments similar to the environmental extremes encountered by soldiers during Operation Anaconda. In addition to protecting soldiers from weather conditions, the uniform would be designed to protect troops from the effects of chemical or biological weapons.[32]

The Unsealed (Unsealable?) Trap

Ground forces made use of existing technology to become more effective during the latter parts of Operation Anaconda. Relying on thermal imagers, Predator aircraft, and satellite data to locate enemy positions, troops would locate the enemy, relay targets, and call in helicopter or fixed-wing air support to strike the enemy.

The end of the battle, however, raises new issues. Afghan and U.S. forces moved to seal off possible escape routes for enemy fighters although many have questioned the effectiveness of this effort. Military officials report that in contrast to Tora Bora—where the enemy fled—many Al Qaeda and Taliban forces remained in their positions.

Officials, however, are unable to provide much data about how many enemy fighters were killed. It is also difficult to find evidence in support of this military evaluation, leading some to conclude that the enemy once again eluded defeat by quietly withdrawing from the battlefield.[33]

This may currently be unavoidable unless enough ground troops are available to saturate the area because sealing off all possible escape routes from a mountainous environment is a near impossible task and requires a large contingent of ground forces. In addition, it is difficult for military planners to decide where to deploy a containment force. A larger battlefield requires a large containment force, and no matter how large that force may be, it may not be able to overcome the natural advantages that mountainous terrain provides an elusive enemy.

Beyond these lessons, Operation Anaconda and other more limited ground operations have revealed a need for improvements in intratheater airlift capabilities. Specifically, the Army needs to increase its ability to transport aviation forces, such as AH-64 Apache helicopters and UH-60 Black Hawk utility helicopters, within the region. A new transport must be able to fly at higher altitudes for longer time periods and must be able to land in makeshift environments. Army officials support developing a tilt-rotor aircraft called the advanced maneuver transport, which can carry both troops and equipment at high speeds and possibly land them behind enemy lines. During the campaign in Afghanistan, helicopters have flown an average of 600 hours per week.[34]

Other broad lessons drawn from the Army's performance during Operation Anaconda and the rest of the war have been announced by Secretary of the Army Thomas White. Evaluating the campaign in Afghanistan, he argued that the fighting situations there indicated that the service is headed in the correct direction when it comes to transformation. Specifically, White stated that the fighting in Afghanistan has shown the versatility of the Army and the need for a balanced force structure. He also cited joint operations of the Army and other services as being a key to decisive victories. From White's perspective, the fighting in Afghanistan has proved that joint operations can be extremely successful.[35] Senior U.S. Army officers, however, are less sanguine. They feel the USA, USAF, and the USN still find it difficult to fully coordinate in close air support, and they indicate there were serious decision-making delays and problems in the flow of national and tactical intelligence.

Communications, Bandwidth, and Satellite Capacity Lessons

While the mountainous terrain of the Shah-i-Kot region was posing numerous physical challenges for U.S. forces to overcome, the environment was also revealing several problems with communications. Soldiers could not rely on line-of-sight communications equipment and had to turn to more expensive and less available military and commercial satellite communications. At the same time, this battle and other experiences in Afghanistan showed that critical aspects of the U.S. national security communications system—such as the Defense Satellite Communications System (DSCS), Milstar, UHF follow-ons, National Reconnaissance Office (NRO) relays, and the National Aeronautics and Space Administration (NASA) Tracking and Data Relay Satellite System (TDRSS) spacecraft—are still stovepiped and lack proper integration. This seems to be true of the designs for the new, advanced EHF and Wideband Gapfiller programs.[36]

This has led to a coordinated effort under the office of the National Security Space Architect (NSSA) by seven teams from each of the key agencies, including the NRO and the National Security Agency (NSA). Improving this aspect of force transformation has been given high priority, and new programs could start to see funding in 2003. The program will be evolutionary and emphasize field use and access across a wide range of channels as well as the integration of the transmission of secure data from NASA, NRO, NSA, and the Defense Department. At present, U.S. forces often have to use two to four different terminals to talk to two to four different satellites in a situation where a single laptop could do the same job. Key new technologies like Lasercom (a satellite-to-ground communications link) are also just beginning to come into service, and there are still no UAV links to the DSCS and Milstar systems. Milstar II is coming into service and will ease some problems but will scarcely serve as a substitute for an integrated systems architecture. Current systems are also particularly weak in rapidly transmitting encrypted imagery.[37]

This situation was made worse by a much broader problem in satellite bandwidth capacity. U.S. military had earlier calculated a far faster growth in commercial satellite capacity than actually took place—some 275 launches actually took place versus the 675 the military had expected. As a result, the Afghan conflict became the first practical case where a lack of bandwidth began to inhibit U.S. communications and ISR capabilities. The U.S. military calculates a need for a total of some 16 gigabits per second in a major theater war by 2010—some 208,000 simultaneous phone calls. Actual military capacity might be little more than half that, creating much higher reliance on commercial communications satellite capacity that may not be available.[38]

Joint and Remote Command Lessons

In some instances, a complicated command structure—dispersed over a wide area with key links in the United States—added to communications problems. CENTCOM did not decide to create a joint task force headquarters until May 2002, when one was created at Bagram.[39] In fact, a number of reports—including an analysis of the course of the war by the USMC—seem to have concluded that CENTCOM's headquarters in Tampa, Florida, some 7,000 miles away, was too far away to coordinate operations in Afghanistan.[40] (In February 2002, the top Marine general commanding operations in Afghanistan moved closer to the theater—from Hawaii to Bahrain).[41]

Although Operation Anaconda was a joint operation, Special Forces from each service were not under joint command. Information relayed from one group of forces to a commander sometimes did not get relayed back out into the field to another group of forces. Overall, however, observers believe that the type of mission conducted by forces in Operation Anaconda indicates the need for higher-bandwidth, more closely linked communication systems that will provide ground forces with up-to-date information on enemy and friendly positions. Analysts also have urged the Army to upgrade its common operational picture, which currently provides UAV imagery of ongoing operations to the commanders. The key to using such technology effectively lies not simply in mainstreaming the collection process but also in training officers to analyze it rapidly and adapt their mission plans as needed.[42]

In their evaluations of the intelligence operation that assisted the military in planning and executing Operation Anaconda, U.S. military officers argued that, despite some inaccuracies, human intelligence played a pivotal role in the success of the mission. Lt. Col. Dave Gray, chief of operations for Operation Anaconda, noted the importance of combining human intelligence with other technical sources. He said that human intelligence was used to confirm observations from surveillance aircraft. Noting the surprisingly fierce resistance that U.S. forces faced during the first days of Anaconda, Gray also argued that limitations in technical intelligence gathering create a continued need for accurate human intelligence, both before and during a battle.[43]

Media Management and Coordination Issues

Information dominance presents other issues. The initial problems encountered by U.S. forces at the start of Operation Anaconda presented media management problems for the U.S. Defense Department. Information coming from both the battlefield and briefings was often sketchy, constantly changing, and, at times, inaccurate. Reporters were not permitted to move close to the fighting, creating a situation in which the media became dependent on secondhand accounts of the unfolding battle.

Military officials and commanders also did not properly explain and educate the media about the rationale behind rotating troops in and out of combat. While many reporters interpreted troop rotations as a sign of military weakness, the rotations were in reality related to the challenges of conducting military operations at such a high altitude. Unnamed military officers who complained of the inadequate use of airpower ignored the economical and tactical realities and capabilities of precision guided munitions. Although the inaccurate and confused reports in the media did not derail the mission, they did create further problems for the Defense Department and the military commanders at a time when they had more pressing issues to worry about. Therefore, managing a clear and accurate flow of information to the media remains an important element of any military operation.[44]

THE CHANGING NATURE OF JOINT WARFARE AND COMBINED ARMS MIX

Virtually every major recent war has shown the growing value of joint operations and of integrating land-air-sea operations in ways adapted to the needs of a given conflict. Like Kosovo, the Afghan conflict has shown that a combination of precision air and missile strike capability, coupled to greatly improved intelligence and targeting systems, can provide much of the heavy firepower in some contingencies that previously had to be handled by artillery and armor.

Part of the shift toward precision has been shown in table 2 on page 11. The shift toward precision is also indicated by the fact that some 6,700 of the 12,000 air weapons—56 percent of the total—that the United States dropped by December 7, 2001, were precision guided. Later estimates indicate that roughly 10,000 weapons were precision weapons; this was out of a total of 18,000—still 56 percent—dropped by early February. This compares with the fact that 35 percent of the 24,000 weapons dropped during the Kosovo campaign in 1999 were precision guided.[45]

As of June 2002, the percentage of precision guided weapons used increased to roughly 60 percent of total munitions, and military officials estimated their accuracy to be roughly 90 percent.[46] It is also worth noting that the ability to correct the dispersal of unguided submunitions for wind and the greatly improved navigation and targeting capabilities also made the delivery of unguided weapons far more precise than it had been in the past.

It is dangerous to overgeneralize because much in both Kosovo and Afghanistan depended on near-supremacy in the air and the ability to engage enemy ground forces in ways in which they could make only limited use or no use of their armor and artillery against U.S. and allied forces—aside from targeting local allies and proxies. Nevertheless, the nature of the air-land battle seems to have evolved significantly, even in terms of the standards of a comparatively recent conflict like Kosovo.[47]

Yet, even if the opponent had had more serious military capabilities, U.S. and British land forces would have had the time to spend several weeks winning air superiority and carrying out the SEAD mission. They could also have added more attack helicopters and gunships to the battle and, possibly, lighter and more mobile artillery and armor—although this presented equipment, lift, and mobility problems for both the Army and Marine Corps. (The Army lacks sufficient light armored vehicles [LAVs] and even ATVs for its Special Forces, and Marine Corps light mechanized forces are still tied more to amphibious missions than to projection by airlift.)

The United States and Britain could also have added more highly trained Special Forces elements, forward air controllers, and experts with local language and cultural skills. Such forces obviously cannot substitute for heavy ground forces in many contingencies, but it is important to note that the Afghan war, per se, is not an argument for lighter tanks and artillery and lighter and more projectable mechanized ground forces. This poses an obvious challenge in restructuring the Marine Corps for operations in the Middle East and possibly in the relative roles of the Marine Corps and the Army.

An advanced communications network, capable of transmitting data among unmanned and manned sensor aircraft, ground forces, combat aircraft, and commanders, is critical to the success of modern joint operations. The fighting in Afghanistan marks a step forward in the development of such a seamless communications system. It is important, however, to note that the U.S. experience in Afghanistan indicates that it may well be a decade or more away from developing all of the right equipment, tactics, and procedures. The enemy in Afghanistan did not have the technological capabilities to interfere with and disable that system. Indeed, while the fighting in Afghanistan shows us that a communications network that integrates information from many different forces is feasible in a nonhostile environment, it has not proved whether such a communications network can withstand an electronic or physical assault from a more advanced foe.[48]

The Value of Strike Range and Endurance in Power Projection

Aircraft range is of limited importance when forward bases are available, but the United States initially could not deploy combat aircraft into bases in Central Asia and Pakistan and had no bases available in Pakistan. The United States did acquire such capabilities over time; it was able to build up a major facility in the forward area at Bagram Air Base in Afghanistan, at Ganci Air Base—named for a New York City firefighter—near the Manas Airport in Kyrgyzstan, and in Pakistan.[49] This lack of forward basing initially limited U.S. attack helicopter operations and meant that shorter-range aircraft like the A-10 and AV-8 were committed only after the fall of Kabul. It was a key factor that forced F-18s, F-14s, and other fighters to fly extremely long missions from carriers in the Indian Ocean and a heavy reliance on refueling as well as long-range bombers.

The fact that the United States could deploy so many fighters at such long distances early in the war, and refuel and maintain them over time, is a considerable achievement. It is not, however, a substitute for aircraft range, and the conditions in Afghanistan showed that the ability to loiter over a target area could be equally important. The range of many U.S. fighters and strike fighters is, however, marginal for such missions. This could also be a problem other areas, like the Persian Gulf, where access to adequate basing is uncertain. In some ways, U.S. airpower is still too divided into fighters best suited for European and littoral operations and long-range bombers. Afghanistan is a warning that the range and endurance of the U.S. strike fighter fleet may be inadequate and that the United States may have left a range gap between strike fighter and bomber.

The conflict in Afghanistan also provided another lesson in the vital importance of midair refueling operations and U.S. tanker forces. However, of the USAF's fleet of 545 KC-135 refueling aircraft, 130 were grounded as of April 2002 owing to structural problems and other maintenance issues. This has led to a debate over the need to replace the aircraft although most should still have substantial flying life. The USAF is currently examining leasing up to 100 modified Boeing 767 aircraft to decrease the demands on refueling tankers, but a long-term solution that reduces overall dependence on USAF refueling assets has yet to be developed. Such a solution will be necessary to ensure future U.S. power projection capabilities, especially in conflicts where the battlefield is located far from U.S. aircraft bases.[50]

Stealth and aircraft range also have advantages. While the stealth characteristics of the B-2 had only marginal value in this war, Afghanistan is also a warning that long-range stealth capabilities may be far more critical in the future. Enemies with advanced air defense systems are not going to let conventional fighters loiter over the battlefield or refuel.

To refuel, F/A-18s and F-14s were forced to descend to 17,000 feet to refuel. After refueling and returning to their previous altitude, the aircraft had used almost as much fuel as had just been added to their tanks. Aircraft like the A-10 and AV-8B needed forward deployment to have sufficient range and time over target. The United States may also find that not all countries are as willing to help as Pakistan and the nations of Central Asia have been. A long-range stealth capability is necessary to allow U.S. airpower to intrude through the air space of third countries.[51]

At the same time, both the United States and Britain have drawn the lesson from Afghanistan that permissive air environments, new sensor and targeting systems, and long-range precision-strike systems allow older long-range slow fliers, like the P-3 and the British Nimrod, to be armed and used as delivery platforms for long-range precision guided munitions. Even tankers and transport aircraft might be reconfigured for use in strike roles. The P-3, for example, was designed for maritime surveillance and antisubmarine warfare missions but was used by the SEALs as a land-based observation plane; with its data links to the Predator and E-8, it provided real-time reconnaissance during battles like Shah-i-Kot and Operation Anaconda.[52]

Older aircraft can also be modified to assist in ISR activities, as the U.S. Navy used the P-3 Orion maritime patrol aircraft in support of special operations forces on the ground in Afghanistan. Taking advantage of the upgrades in communications, radar, and sensor capabilities made to aircraft as part of the P-3 Antisurface Warfare

Improvement Program (AIP), the Navy used P-3s to gather ISR information that was then transmitted directly to special operations forces on the ground. SEAL teams could not only download information from the P-3; they could also upload target information and coordinates to the P-3, which in turn would transmit the information to strike aircraft.[53]

To enhance ISR, the USAF modified existing aircraft by placing communications pallets on KC-135 tanker aircraft. These modified aircraft communicated with the CAOC in Saudi Arabia and relayed battlefield information to F-15 aircraft. Secretary of the Air Force James G. Roche stated that the "smart tanker" worked well; consequently, the USAF plans to modify 40 of its current KC-135s so that they can further enhance battlefield communications.[54]

Common Base Operations

In clear need of review is the lack of effective U.S. planning for common base operations support (BOS) in joint doctrine/procedures. Some analysts feel the integration of conventional land forces and special operations forces at the support level at austere bases was not a pretty story and helped lead to a surprisingly slow buildup of SOF teams in Afghanistan. This will probably surprise many people, given what was accomplished.

There seems good reason to question whether each service or service component should rely as much as it does on having its own base support, as is the case today. The United States also needs to examine carefully the tendency to "gold plate" the basing capabilities for some combat and support elements while leaving others austere, and the tendency to use different levels of force protection for different services and components. Specialization is one thing, duplication is another; and joint basing may offer significant savings as well as increase the speed of power projection.

THE VALUE OF COALITION WARFARE AND
MISSION-ORIENTED INTEROPERABILITY

Recent wars have repeatedly demonstrated the value of coalition warfare in every aspect of operations from power projection to combat. The Afghan conflict, however, is interesting because light, highly trained allied forces like the British Special Air Service (SAS) proved they could be highly effective without expensive high-technology equipment, standardization, and interoperability. Similarly, relatively primitive allied local ground forces could be very effective substitutes for U.S. ground forces when given the support of U.S. Special Forces and advisers and effective air and missile strike capability. This is a lesson that emerged in a different way from the role that the Kosovo Liberation Army and other Kosovar forces played in Kosovo.

Rethinking the Emphasis on High-Cost Forces and Force Improvements

The U.S. and British experience in Afghanistan may indicate that the United States and NATO have overstressed the high-technology and high-investment aspects of coalition warfare and interoperability, and may have paid too little attention to the value of being able to draw on a pool of highly trained lighter forces, like the SAS or their Australian, Canadian, German, and other equivalents.

The same may be true of the value of using limited, but highly trained, numbers of advisers and forward air controllers and targeters on the ground, along with rapid transfers of low- and medium-technology arms, to strengthen local forces. It seems fair to say that in the past the United States has paid more attention to seeking "technological clones" or doing the task alone instead of using its specialized high-technology strengths in ways that make it easier to operate with less-well-equipped Western and regional allied forces. This may well have been a too narrow, if not wrong, approach to coalition warfare and interoperability in many mission areas.

The Growing Role of Allied Coalition Forces

Significant problems arose in initial deployment of allied forces. The basing, transportation, and support systems available at the start of the Afghan campaign limited U.S. ability to accept allied forces. So did the lack of language training, command-and-control assets, and cross-training in the use of U.S. ISR equipment and battle management (BM) techniques as well as problems in combat rescue and force protection capabilities. Most allied forces lacked strategic mobility and sustainability, and the United States was not organized to use many of the assets other countries offered. The lack of a clear U.S. nation-building plan and prior allied planning for such a mission also meant that the United States was relatively slow to recognize the importance of nation building and peacekeeping support.

The situation changed radically as time went on, however, and the value of allied forces became clear. By June 2002, 20 nations had deployed more than 16,000 troops to CENTCOM's region of responsibility. In Afghanistan alone, coalition partners contributed more than 7,000 troops to Operation Enduring Freedom and to the International Security Assistance Force (ISAF) in Kabul—making up more than half of the 14,000 non-Afghan forces in Afghanistan.

The following list of allied forces supporting the United States as of June 2002 illustrates both the flexibility that coalition operations can play as well as the political and military value of what are often small contributions.[55]

Australia

- Special operations forces currently in Afghanistan performing the full spectrum of their missions; second rotation of these forces has recently occurred and demonstrates Australia's ongoing support of operations in Afghanistan;

- Deployed two dedicated KB-707 aircraft to Manas, Kyrgyzstan; deployment includes a significant number of support personnel;

- Air force is filling a key wing leadership position (operations group commander) at Manas;

- Fighter aircraft deployed to perform combat air patrol (CAP) missions at Diego Garcia in support of Pacific Command; highlights Australia's broader commitment to the war on terror and the significant relationship Australia and the United States share across a number of areas of responsibility (AORs);

- Deployed three ships to the CENTCOM AOR supporting naval operations: HMAS *Manoora,* HMAS *Canberra,* and HMAS *Newcastle;* conducting maritime interception operations in the Arabian Gulf and enforcing UN sanctions against Iraq;

- National command element is forward deployed in the region, providing command and control for deployed forces; and

- Suffered the first non-U.S. military fatality on February 16, 2002; Sgt. Andrew Russell was killed in action as the result of a land mine explosion; previously another member of Australia's special forces—who is recovering in Australia—lost his foot in another land mine incident.

Belgium

- Providing one officer to the Coalition Intelligence Center at CENTCOM and one officer to the Regional Air Movement Control Center to serve as deputy chief of operations;

- Air force C-130 aircraft delivered a high-protein food supplement (UNIMIX) from Denmark to Dushanbe, Tajikistan, and an A-310 (Airbus) delivered 250,000 vaccinations for children under the UNICEF program;

- Led the largest multinational humanitarian assistance mission, which included Belgium, Spain, Netherlands, and Norway; mission provided 90 metric tons of UNIMIX to feed starving children in Afghanistan and set the standard for follow-on humanitarian assistance operations;

- Contributed four people to Operation Noble Eagle supporting U.S. homeland security efforts; they are currently at Tinker Air Force Base; and

- In contribution to the ISAF, a Belgian C-130 with air crew and maintenance crew (25 people)—working on a one-month rotation schedule—arrived in Karachi on April 10, 2002; they will stay in Karachi and execute part of the 400 dedicated C-130 flight hours for ISAF.

Bulgaria

- Will provide basing and overflight rights upon request—standard clearance authority for overflights;
- Provided basing for six KC-135 aircraft to support humanitarian flights into Afghanistan during November and December 2001; and
- Provided a 40-person nuclear, biological, chemical (NBC) decontamination unit to support ISAF in Kabul.

Canada

- First coalition task group to arrive in CENTCOM AOR;
- Currently has 2,025 personnel in the CENTCOM AOR (1,100 land, 225 air and 700 naval personnel); to date, 3,400 personnel have deployed in support of Operation Enduring Freedom;
- Naval forces have been engaged in maritime interception operations (MIO), leadership interdiction operations (LIO), escort duties, and general maritime surveillance between the North Arabian Gulf and the North Arabian Sea; seven ships deployed to Operation Enduring Freedom from October 2001 to April 2002;
- Air Command CC-150 Polaris (Airbus) and three CC-130 (Hercules) aircraft have conducted strategic and tactical airlift; have moved more than 7.8 million pounds of freight to date;
- Two CP-140 Aurora (P3C) aircraft employed in MIO/LIO as part of Carrier Task Force 57;

- Eighty-four missions and 746 flight hours logged to date; organic helicopter assets have flown 930 missions for more than 2,900 hours;
- Special operations forces currently in Afghanistan performing the full spectrum of missions;
- HMCS *Toronto*, while operating in the North Arabian Sea, intercepted a small vessel laden with 4,500 pounds of hashish (valued at more than $60 million); its crew abandoned the vessel during the interception; cargo and vessel were subsequently destroyed; and
- Light infantry battle group deployed as part of Task Force Rakkasan with 828 personnel and 12 Coyote armored reconnaissance vehicles; forces have been deployed to Kandahar for security and combat operations; successes to date include:
  - Leadership of Operation Harpoon, March 13–16, 2002; investigated 30 caves and four mortar positions; action resulted in three enemy killed in action;
  - Conducted patrol on March 18, 2002, in the Kandahar region that uncovered a cache of weapons (including three thermobaric launchers);
  - Continuing to conduct civil-military cooperation (CIMIC) efforts in the Kandahar area; and
  - Provided the quick reaction force that deployed from Kandahar to secure the site of the Apache helicopter that crashed on April 10, 2002.

Czech Republic

- Representatives arrived at CENTCOM on November 9, 2001; currently three Czech personnel at CENTCOM;
- Approximately 250 personnel deployed to Camp Doha, Kuwait, to perform local training as well as AOR-wide consequence management (CM) support; and
- Offered to donate 1,000 military uniforms to support the Afghan National Army.

Denmark

- Air force is providing one C-130 aircraft with 77 crew and support personnel;
- Air force will deploy four F-16 aircraft in an air-to-ground role with pilots and support personnel in October; these assets are on standby in Denmark;
- Approximately 100 special operations forces personnel have deployed to the AOR as part of a multinational unit under U.S. command; because of rotation of forces, the number at present is approximately 65; and
- Suffered three killed and three wounded in action supporting ISAF operations.

Egypt

- Provided overflight permission for all U.S. and coalition forces; and
- Representatives arrived at CENTCOM on November 28, 2001; currently three Egyptian personnel at CENTCOM.

Estonia

- Approved unconditional overflight and landing rights for all U.S. and coalition partners;
- Offered two explosive detection dog teams for airbase operations; and
- Offered 10 cargo handlers as part of Danish contingent deployed to Manas, Kyrgyzstan.

Finland

- Military liaison team at CENTCOM continues to concentrate especially on civil-military operations with an objective to facilitate cooperation and coordination between ISAF, Operation Enduring Freedom, and UN operations in Afghanistan;

- Assisting the Afghan administration, nongovernmental humanitarian organizations, and military forces in Afghanistan in an effort to promote the long-term reconstruction of the country; and
- Providing the largest CIMIC unit in Kabul in support of ISAF; unit currently consists of nearly 50 officers.

France

- Air force, deploying C-160 and C-130 aircraft to Dushanbe, Tajikistan, has provided humanitarian assistance as well as national and coalition airlift support;
- Two KC-135 aircraft have deployed to Manas, Kyrgyzstan, to provide aerial refueling;
- Six Mirage 2000 fighter aircraft have also deployed to Manas to provide close air support capability;
- Engineers helped construct runways, a tent city, and a munitions storage facility at Manas;
- Provided airfield security (with dogs), a field mess unit, a deployable weather bureau, and a civil-military operations team;
- Deployed an infantry company to Mazar-i-Sharif to provide area security up to December 2001;
- Two officers are currently serving as air coordinators at the Regional Air Movement Control Center;
- Atlantique aircraft are deployed in Djibouti under national control and are participating daily in ISR missions;
- Providing its only carrier battle group to support combat operations in the North;
- Aircraft from Arabian Sea battle group have flown more than 2,000 hours for Operation Enduring Freedom to support the coalition with air reconnaissance, strike, and airborne early warning (AEW) missions; naval contribution accounts for approximately 24 percent of France's entire naval forces;

- Only coalition country to be flying fighter aircraft from Manas airfield in Kyrgyzstan;

- Mirage and tanker aircraft actively supported the coalition during Operation Anaconda in March and are maintaining their full combat and support capabilities for further operations; and

- World Health Organization, the French embassy, Loma Linda (an NGO), and French forces (500 personnel) inserted into ISAF are working to make major improvements—equipment, books and a new curriculum—to the Kabul Medical Institute; the student body of about 2,800 includes 544 women.

Germany

- Approximately 2,560 German personnel are currently operating within the CENTCOM AOR;

- Special operations forces are currently in Afghanistan performing the full spectrum of their missions;

- Navy has had three frigates, one fast patrol boat group (five units), and four supply ships operating out of Djibouti, in the Gulf of Aden area, since January 2002; two German Sea King helicopters are based in Djibouti;

- A-310 (Airbus) aircraft is on alert in Germany for use as a medevac platform;

- One battalion-sized infantry task force operating in Kabul as part of ISAF operations; this force is supported by an air transport element operating out of Uzbekistan;

- USAID and Coalition Joint Civil-Military Operations Task Force (CJCMOTF) are working on a plan to employ widows of Afghan war veterans;

- Afghan war widows to make uniforms for the Kabul police force, a microindustry proposal made possible by a German contribution of 10 million euros to help train and equip the police force; and

- First time German ships and maritime patrol aircraft have been operationally involved in a Middle East deployment in more than 50 years; three German maritime patrol aircraft began conducting reconnaissance operations from Mombasa, Kenya; Germany conducted HA flights to support relief efforts for earthquake victims in Afghanistan.

Greece

- Frigate *Psara* has been in CENTCOM's AOR since March 15, conducting operations under the operational control of coalition forces maritime component commander (CFMCC); this frigate is of Meko type and is one of the most sophisticated vessels in Greece's inventory; it carries a crew of 189, one S-70 BA Aegean Hawk helicopter, and one special forces team; it has the ability to perform and execute a variety of missions and will be replaced in three months by another frigate of the same type, so there will be constant Greek naval presence in the area of interest;
- Facilities of Greek naval base and airbase of Souda, Crete, as well as other basing settlements across the country, are used as forward logistics sites to support ships and aircraft moving in the area;
- One air force officer is going to be assigned as an operations officer of the Regional Air Movement Control Center (RAMCC) in Afghanistan, and one navy liaison officer will deploy to Bahrain;
- Active in ISAF operations:
  - One engineer company of 123 men and 64 engineering vehicles has been operating in Kabul;
  - Two C-130 transport aircraft with a support security team of 56 personnel have deployed to Karachi, Pakistan, for tactical airlift in support of ISAF operations; and
  - Staff officers have been assigned to permanent joint headquarters (PJHQ) in Great Britain and to ISAF headquarters in Kabul;

- NATO operations in the Mediterranean Sea include:
  - One frigate and one countermine ship have been conducting surveillance and mine-sweeping operations, respectively, in east Mediterranean Sea; and
  - Two more vessels and a number of air force sorties offered in support of Operation Active Endeavor against international terrorism.

India

- Provided frigate for escorting coalition shipping through the Strait of Malacca;
- Made shipyards available for coalition ship repairs; and
- Opened ports for naval port calls.

Italy

- Air force is planning to deploy one C-130 plus one Boeing-707 to Manas airfield following initial force rotation;
- Self-deployment of a 43-man engineer team to Bagram for the repairing of the runway took place May 10–22, 2002;
- Personnel are committed to both Operation Enduring Freedom and ISAF operations; a 400-man regimental task force was deployed on January 15, 2002, to provide ISAF area and site security in the Kabul area;
- Providing three C-130s (two operating from Abu Dhabi) and is leasing one B-707, one AN-124, and one IL-76 in support of ISAF;
- Provided its only carrier battle group to support combat operations in the northern Arabian Sea;
- Deployed more than 13 percent of its entire naval forces for use in Operation Enduring Freedom; the De La Penne Group (one destroyer and one frigate) relieved the carrier battle group on March 15, 2002;

- Frigate *Euro* transited the Suez Canal on May 8 to relieve both combatants on station;
- Moved more than 17,000 pounds (27 cubic meters) of supplies and equipment from Brindisi to Islamabad, Pakistan, on March 19, 2002; supplies and equipment included a forklift and equipment from the World Food Program; and
- On April 18, 2002, aircraft and security force transported without incident the former king of Afghanistan, Muhammad Zahir Shah, and the leader of the Afghan Interim Authority, Hamid Karzai, from Rome to Kabul.

Japan

- Provided fleet-refueling capability, placing two refueling-replenishment ships and three support-protection destroyers in the AOR; through mid-May 2002, this force has conducted 75 at-sea replenishments of coalition ships and provided 34.1 million gallons of F-76 fuel to U.S. and UK vessels;
- Also as of mid-May 2002, six C-130 aircraft had completed 51 missions consisting of 166 sorties with 773 tons of cargo and 123 passengers in support of resupply and transport requirements within the Pacific Command (PACOM) AOR; and
- On May 17, 2002, government approved a six-month extension of the basic plan authorizing Japan's Self Defense Forces to continue these efforts.

Jordan

- Aardvark mine-clearing unit and personnel are currently deployed to Kandahar and have cleared mines from more than 70,000 square meters in both Bagram and Kandahar;
- Provided basing and overflight permission for all U.S. and coalition forces; and
- As of May 16, 2002, Jordanian hospital in Mazar-i-Sharif helped 57,536 patients:

- military: 989; civilian: women – 22,297, men – 18,861, children – 15,389; and
- Performed 683 surgeries.

Kazakhstan

- Signed an agreement with the United States in July 2002 permitting U.S. and coalition aircraft to make emergency landings and refuel at the international airport in Almaty.[56]

Kuwait

- Provided basing and overflight permission for all U.S. and coalition forces; and
- Representatives arrived at CENTCOM on February 14, 2002; three personnel currently at CENTCOM support operations in Operation Enduring Freedom.

Kyrgyzstan

- As part of backfill, has offered to double (to two infantry companies) its contributions to the Stabilization Force (SFOR) in Bosnia and Herzegovina and more than double (to 25 soldiers) its Kosovo Peacekeeping Force (KFOR) contributions.

Latvia

- Approved use of airspace, airfields, and ports for global war on terrorism; and
- Offered 10 cargo handlers as part of Danish contingent deployed to Manas.

Lithuania

- Approved use of airspace, airfields, and ports for global war on terrorism;
- Offered 10 cargo handlers as part of Danish contingent deployed to Manas, Kyrgyzstan;

- Scheduled to deploy an ambulance with medics as part of a Czech Republic contingent; and

- Offered SOF platoon, military divers, translators, minesweeper, aircraft, and maintenance support to SFOR and KFOR.

Malaysia

- Approved all requests for overflight clearance since September 11; and

- Provided access to Malaysian intelligence.

Netherlands

- Air force KDC-10 is currently deployed to Al Udeid, Qatar; to date, C-130 aircraft have completed three HA flights under national flag;

- Will deploy one C-130 aircraft to Manas to assist with the logistics hub movement of cargo from that airport;

- F-16s will be deployed to Manas in October 2002;

- Two naval frigates are currently operating in the CENTCOM AOR; other naval ships, along with air force P-3s, will relieve U.S. units in the Southern Command AOR;

- One person working as a planning officer at the RAMCC;

- Contributed 220 troops to ISAF; and

- On March 27, 2002, officer from Netherlands arrived at the RAMCC.

New Zealand

- SAS troops work alongside the forces of other nations in Afghanistan; they fill an important role as part of the international effort to stabilize the area;

- Provided logistics and humanitarian airlift support in Afghanistan with air force C-130 aircraft; aircraft were made available to help move the backlog of equipment and supplies needed for Operation Enduring Freedom;

- Seven-person air loading team (ALT) deployed to support ISAF; and
- Will deploy up to eight officers to staff the ISAF headquarters.

Norway

- Hydrema 910 mine-clearing vehicles and personnel have been responsible for clearing more than 640,000 square meters of terrain on Kandahar and Bagram airfields and surrounding areas since their deployment on January 1, 2002;
- SOF self-deployed into Afghanistan and are currently providing a full spectrum of missions there;
- Air force C-130 aircraft are providing intratheater tactical airlift support and support to Operation Enduring Freedom, operating from Manas airbase; on a national basis, the C-130 has conducted resupply missions for Norwegian SOF forces and humanitarian assistance missions to Afghanistan;
- Will deploy F-16s to Manas in October;
- SOF exploitation missions have yielded valuable intelligence;
- Provided 15 hardened vehicles ($1.5 million) that are currently supporting SOF missions and providing leadership transport; and
- In unified effort to rebuild the Afghan army, Norway has donated personal items and equipment for a 700-person light infantry battalion.

Pakistan

- Provided basing and overflight permission for all U.S. and coalition forces;
- Deployed a large number of troops along the Afghanistan border in support of Operation Enduring Freedom;

- Spent a large portion of its logistical reserves to support the coalition, a very significant contribution in light of Pakistan's economic difficulties and self-defense support requirements;

- Representatives arrived at CENTCOM on March 14, 2002; five at CENTCOM in mid-2002; and

- Inter-Services Intelligence (ISI) has helped in various phases of operations.

Philippines

- Provided landing rights and base support for U.S. aircraft;

- Granted unconditional blanket overflight clearance; and

- Offered medical and logistical support for Operation Enduring Freedom.

Poland

- Combat engineers and logistics platoon forces recently deployed to Bagram via Kabul;

- Eight AN-124 flights coordinated with the RAMCC to move these forces (a large and costly operation for the Poles); and

- Since their arrival in mid-March, these engineers have cleared mines from more than 4,000 square meters of land.

Portugal

- Representatives arrived at CENTCOM on December 13, 2001;

- Currently under ISAF control, a medical team of eight people and a C-130 with a maintenance team of 15 people.

Republic of Korea

- Naval vessel transported more than 1,000 tons of critical construction material from Singapore to Diego Garcia to support the need for Operation Enduring Freedom building materials;

- Pledged more than $45 million to aid in the reconstruction of Afghanistan;

- Deployed a level-two hospital to Manas; and

- Air force C-130s have flown eighteen flights between Seoul and Diego Garcia as well as five flights to Islamabad; transported more than 45 tons of humanitarian relief supplies valued at $12 million.

Romania

- On September 19, 2001, Romanian parliament approved basing and overflight permission for all U.S. and coalition partners;

- Three liaison officers arrived at CENTCOM on December 10, 2001; one is working in the coalition intelligence center;

- Will deploy one infantry battalion into Afghanistan; in addition, one infantry mountain company, one NBC company, four MiG-21 Lancer aircraft, and medical personnel have been offered;

- Deployed for ISAF one military police platoon and one C-130 aircraft;

- Delivered a large quantity of training equipment for the Afghan national guard;

- Parliament recently approved the deployment of a 405-person motorized infantry battalion, a 70-person NBC company, and 10 staff officers; and

- Donated the following items in support of the ANA: 1,000 AK-47 assault rifles, 300,000 rounds of ammunition, magazines, and cleaning sets.

Russia

- Started providing humanitarian assistance to the population of Afghanistan in October 2001;

- Supported humanitarian assistance operations by transporting more than 420,296 tons of food commodities, 2,198 tons of medicines, 15,282 beds, 1,200 heaters, 13 mini–electric power stations, 780 tents, 11,000 blankets, 49,674 bedding kits, 11,000 pieces of kitchen utensils, and 9 tons of detergents;

- In December 2001, Russian personnel started reconstruction of the Salang tunnel connecting northern and southern provinces of Afghanistan; in January 2002, the Salang tunnel was officially opened for regular traffic;

- In January 2002, as a result of a joint Russian-German project, pontoon passage across Pianj River was put into service; together with Salang tunnel it allowed the organization of a continuous route from Tajikistan to central region of Afghanistan for delivery of international humanitarian assistance;

- Provided first coalition hospital in Kabul on November 29, 2001; hospital treated more than 6,000 patients before Russia turned facility over to the local population on January 25, 2002;

- On March 29, 2002, EMERCOM, Russia's emergency response organization, deployed mobile hospital to Nakhreen and began medical assistance to victims of earthquake;

- EMERCOM has delivered over 100 metric tons of HA supplies to the Nakhreen area, including provisions, medicines, and means for cleaning water; and

- Rescue teams have conducted search-and-rescue operations throughout the area.

Slovakia

- On September 18, 2001, Slovakia notified the United States that it would grant blanket overflight and basing rights to all coalition partners;

- Dispatched a liaison officer to CENTCOM headquarters on March 10, 2002; and

- Will deploy engineering unit into Afghanistan; in addition, has offered special forces regiment, NBC reconnaissance units, and a mobile field hospital.

Spain

- Deployed one P-3B to Djibouti, two C-130s to Manas, and one C-130 that accomplished its mission and is back in Spain;

- Two naval frigates and one support ship deployed to the CENTCOM AOR to support continued operations in Operation Enduring Freedom;

- Maritime patrol aircraft began conducting reconnaissance operations from French base in Djibouti; deployed search-and-rescue helicopters to Manas on April 12; and

- As of May 16, 2002, the Spanish hospital in Bagram has helped 6,343 patients:
  - Military: 1,110; civilian: women – 1,261, men – 1,670, children – 2,302; and
  - Performed 66 surgeries.

Sweden

- Representatives arrived at CENTCOM on March 28, 2002; currently two personnel at CENTCOM.

Turkey

- Provided basing and overflight permission for all U.S. and coalition forces;

- One officer scheduled to work as planning officer at the RAMCC;

- First coalition country to provide KC-135 aerial refueling support for U.S. aircraft during transits to CENTCOM AOR; and

- As of June 20, 2002, assumed position as lead nation for the second phase of ISAF operations in Afghanistan.[57]

United Arab Emirates

- Representatives arrived at CENTCOM on November 1, 2001; currently three personnel at CENTCOM.

United Kingdom

- Representatives arrived at CENTCOM on September 18, 2001; currently 38 personnel at CENTCOM; UK also has staff attached to every major U.S. component command;

- Senior British major general serves as deputy commander for all coalition naval forces in theater, responsible for coordinating extensive operations; British forces have participated in MIO and Tomahawk land attack missile (TLAM) operations;

- Royal Air Force provided aircraft throughout the region and contributed high-value assets in the critical areas of aerial refueling, airborne early warning (AEW), and ISR;

- UK ground forces participated in both Operation Enduring Freedom and ISAF missions; company of Royal Marines from 40-Commando deployed to Kabul and contributed to airfield security and mine clearing operations, including provision of special equipment at both Bagram and Kabul airports;

- First nation to send military representatives and campaign planners to CENTCOM;

- Deployed the largest naval task force since the Gulf War to support Operation Enduring Freedom;

- Provided the only coalition TLAM platforms to launch missiles during the commencement of Operation Enduring Freedom hostilities;

- Assumed the lead for the initial ISAF operation; and

- On March 21, 2002, began deployment to Afghanistan of a 1,700-person infantry battle group, built around 45-Commando, Royal Marines; these arctic- and mountain-warfare-trained troops operate as part of a U.S.-led brigade and conduct operations along the Afghanistan-Pakistan border in search of Al Qaeda and Taliban fighters as well as weapons caches; on July 9, 2002, majority of the Royal Marines completed tour of duty in Afghanistan.[58]

Uzbekistan

- Provided basing and overflight permission for U.S. and coalition forces; and

- Representatives arrived at CENTCOM on December 26, 2001; four personnel at CENTCOM.

CLOSING THE SENSOR-TO-SHOOTER LOOP IN NEAR REAL TIME: IMPROVED INTELLIGENCE, TARGETING, PRECISION STRIKE, ASSESSMENT, AND RESTRIKE CAPABILITIES

Regardless of all of the previous issues and reservations, no one can dismiss the major impact on the fighting of new technologies, particularly when the technologies were employed with new tactics and as part of new systems.[59] According to Gen. Tommy Franks, the United States had flown an average of 200 sorties a day in Afghanistan by early February 2002; this compares with 3,000 a day in Desert Storm. In Afghanistan, however, the United States was able to hit roughly the same number of targets per day as it had in Desert Storm.[60] Franks stated that while the United States needed an average of 10 aircraft to take out a target in Desert Storm, a single aircraft could often take out two targets during the fighting in Afghanistan. Unofficial estimates claim that USN aircraft experienced a 70–80 percent success rate in hitting designated targets.[61] Afghanistan demonstrated a much greater surge capability of using precision weapons against a major array of targets. In one case, the United States fired roughly 100 JDAMs in a 20-minute period.[62]

These estimates almost certainly exaggerated U.S. performance. Both the assistant secretary of defense (public affairs) and the preliminary findings of the Department of Defense task force Enduring Look—the U.S. military team examining the lessons of the war—have cautioned that this is the case.[63] Nevertheless, it is clear that major improvements over past wars were made possible by a number of factors including added reliance on precision guided weapons and new abilities of U.S. forces to draw on greatly enhanced ISR capabilities.[64]

The United States was able to link its air and ground forces to power ISR assets. It could provide real-time imagery (PHOTINT) and ELINT data on the movements of enemy and friendly forces. From imagery satellites—U-2s, E-8 JSTARS, RC-135 Rivet Joints, E-3A AWACS, E-2s, P-3s, and UAVs like the Global Hawk and Predator—it could cover and characterize fixed targets as well as cover and target mobile enemy forces with high precision in real time even as they were engaged by Afghan ground forces. Although SIGINT was not automated in a form that allowed the same degree of instant reporting and communication, it too played a role. Advances in U.S. sensors, moving target radars, and synthetic aperture radars also reduced weather and cloud-cover problems.

The United States had the technical capability to communicate these data, including targeting data, to U.S. bombers and strike fighters, Special Forces, other ground forces, and sea-launched cruise missile platforms. This allowed aircraft like the F-16, F-15, AC-130, F-18, B-1, and B-52 to not only operate with near-real-time intelligence but to retarget in flight and in some cases restrike after damage assessment from forces on the ground.[65] At the same time, a family of new, light, ground systems like the joint tactical terminal used by U.S. Special Forces and other ground forces, the components of the integrated broadcast service, new laser illuminators, GPS systems, and satellite uplinks transformed tactical ISR operations in the field.[66]

The U.S. ability to use such data to conduct precision strikes with both precision guided weapons and area ordnance, and then at least partially assess damage as well as retarget and restrike almost immediately, did make use of a wide range of ongoing advances in tactics and technology. The United States was sometimes able to close the loop in conducting air and missile strikes in near real time. The United States also demonstrated an impressive further development of techniques that owe their origins to the use of spotter aircraft and kill boxes in the Gulf War and that were significantly further developed in Kosovo.[67] This time, however, the United States could make far more use of UAVs and got far closer to potential targets.

Tactical encounters between U.S. and Al Qaeda forces have shown it is now possible for airpower to be far more effective and responsive in the close support of missions and for precision weapons to act as a partial substitute for artillery when the enemy does not have high-quality short-range air defenses or large numbers of heavy weapons. A combination of fixed- and rotary-wing aircraft performed such missions well during the fighting at Tora Bora. In the summer of 2002, however, U.S. military officials concede that airpower is of limited use in locating and destroying small, dispersed pockets of Al Qaeda and Taliban fighters. Indeed, rapid surgical strikes by ground troops remain a more effective option for combating a dispersed enemy.[68]

Asset Integration and New Approaches to Land Warfare

One key factor must be borne in mind. The period of the Afghanistan War is still in the early days of net-centric warfare. Far more can be done to improve the integration of U.S. sensors, battle management systems, strike platforms, communications, and use of precision weapons in the future. Many U.S. efforts during the Afghan conflict were improvised, relatively crude, and scarcely set the standard for the level of progress that can be achieved in closing the loop. A number of analysts have since argued that the advances in BM and ISR have reached the point where platforms are less important than achieving a broad fusion of BM-ISR and that precision strike assets can be used to strike as effectively as possible in near real time, regardless of the age of the launch platform.[69]

UAVs are clearly advancing rapidly. Although much depends on the sophistication of the opponent's air and air defense assets, the use of stealth, long-range standoff munitions, UAVs, and UACVs offers a potential way to use such techniques even against sophisticated opponents. At the same time, land systems like the high-mobility artillery rocket system, Netfires, and precision guided artillery shells could provide land firepower capabilities with equal precision fire capability and more mobility and ease of power projection than existing artillery systems. Although development of unmanned ground vehicles (UGVs) lags behind that of UAVs, in part because of the difficult nature of ground navigation, UGVs could offer further enhancements to already existing sensor and weapons platforms.[70]

The result could be what some call "asset integration" and the creation of forces that combine land-air-sea systems into a near-real-time mix of capabilities to target-strike-assess-retarget-and-restrike with an efficiency that has never been previously achieved.[71] It would extend joint warfare and combined arms to a new level.

Senior USA officers also feel that this may be an important key to force transformation for the Army. Instead of using large land forces that can secure their flanks and need heavy armor and artillery, the Army could rely on sensors to avoid surprise and could counter-maneuver before the enemy could react. Air and missile power would substitute for heavy forces in many contingencies, and air mobility would allow rapid maneuvering to strike at the most critical aspects of enemy ground force operations. The result could be smaller, faster, and more effective ground units that would also be much easier and faster to deploy and would require much less logistic and service support.

Impact of UAVs and UCAVs

UAVs have become the focus of much of the attention to technology during the Afghan conflict. The ability of UAVs such as the USAF RQ-4A Global Hawk to see through clouds, detect heat on the ground, and fly at altitudes of up to 65,000 feet for roughly 30 hours provided commanders with near-real-time intelligence. As of June 14, 2002, UAVs had logged 1,000 combat flight hours.[72]

A lack of assets has been a problem, however. The United States possesses only a limited number of the key UAVs involved, and these limits interact with the fact that many of the round-the-clock improvements the United States plans to make in imagery satellites and electronic intelligence satellites have not yet been deployed.[73] The United States currently plans to buy 22 more RQ-1 Predators, at least three more RQ-4 Global Hawks, and 12 Army Shadows but is only beginning to determine with certainty the size of the fleet it will eventually need. A lack of military bandwidth capacity could also be a problem.[74]

Problems exist in the current UAVs and in the ways they are used, however. The Predator has had considerable success: it can fly up to

25,000 feet, can remain on station for more than 24 hours, is equipped with electro-optical and infrared sensors as well as synthetic aperture radar for all-weather and day-night coverage, can carry two Hellfire missiles, has a laser designator to illuminate targets, and has been the first real UCAV to enter U.S. service.[75]

Nevertheless, it remains a troubled system. It largely failed operational testing before the Afghan conflict, with some eight crashes in the six months before the conflict. It cannot take off in severe rain, snow, ice, or fog. Its imagery lacks the definition to find and characterize some types of targets; it is a slow flier (90 mph) that operates best at 10,000 feet, which puts it within range of many forms of light anti-aircraft defense and has led to losses in Afghanistan and Iraq; it has awkward control systems and ergonomics; and each unit (four planes and a ground station) costs about $25 million.[76]

Since the beginning of operations in Afghanistan, two Global Hawk UAVs have crashed. The first of these crashes was attributed to a faulty bolt; the more recent crash, which occurred in July 2002, is still under investigation. The Air Force's remaining Global Hawk UAVs have been grounded until the cause of the second crash can be determined.[77]

Evaluations of the performance in Afghanistan of Predator and other drone aircraft have been mixed. While military commanders cite the Predator's ability to "peer over the hill" and provide imagery of the landscape and layout of enemy forces in future combat zones, they also worry that forces preparing for battle may become too dependent on the data from the Predators and be unprepared to handle nonvisible threats.[78]

During the fighting in March 2002, Predator drones provided live pictures of ongoing combat operations as they evolved in Afghanistan to U.S. military officials in a variety of locations, including the air operations center (AOC) in Saudi Arabia, CENTCOM, the Pentagon, and the CIA. Real-time information can, however, provoke real-time micromanagement. Though such images provided military commanders several thousand miles removed from the field with information as well as a firsthand, never-before-seen view of the battle, the images also caused headaches for the commander of regular U.S.

ground forces in Afghanistan who was overseeing the operation. Throughout the battles in the Shah-i-Kot region, command personnel at higher levels, and operating in other locations, relayed numerous questions and much advice to the commander in the field in an attempt to contribute to the management of unfolding battle. The regional commander responded by posting updates on the progress of the battle on the military's internal computer network.

Nevertheless, the episode reveals the powerful influence that live pictures from the battle zone can have on the ability of the on-site commander to determine and execute a successful battle plan. The last thing the U.S. field commanders need is an overcomplicated chain of command, with officers thousands of miles away from the scene of battle providing armchair advice on the basis of pictures rolling across a television screen. If such imagery is to be used effectively, an effective way of analyzing it and providing feedback to the command on the ground must be developed.[79]

Military officials argue that the Predator could be a far more effective tool if commanders could communicate with the team operating it, much as they do with helicopter pilots and fighter pilots, issuing instructions and calibrating the use of the drone to advance the overall goals of the mission at hand.[80]

The Predator's operational limits have also led to plans to equip it with much more lethal weapons with standoff range, like LOCAAS, and develop a Predator B to replace the existing Predator RQ-1. The Predator B would increase range well over the present 740 kilometers and increase speed from 138 to 253 miles per hour, payload from 450 to 750 pounds, maximum altitude from 25,000 to 45,000 feet, wingspan from 48.7 to 64 feet, and length from 27 to 34 feet.[81] The United States also is seeking to develop an export version for NATO allies.[82]

Despite these problematic limitations, UAVs and UCAVs have clearly proved to be a worthwhile asset in Afghanistan and have reached the development stage where they are able to operate as semiautonomous sensors and weapons platforms.

The Strengths and Weaknesses of Other Platforms

Little reliable detail is yet available on the strengths and weaknesses of the Airborne Warning and Control System (AWACS), JSTARS, U-2, Rivet Joint, P-3, satellite, and other sensor platforms that ultimately have done most of the work in Afghanistan. It is clear from the FY 2003 defense budget submission, however, that funds are being provided to improve virtually every system and that serious attention is being given to adding sensors to aircraft like tankers and adding more sophisticated mixes of sensors to existing aircraft.

The idea of a single platform to perform the functions of the AWACS and JSTARS is also being explored. Similarly, major efforts are being made to improve networking and connectivity. At least some of the data links used to provide real-time retargeting data to aircraft were still relatively crude and had poor ergonomics; avionics and air munitions were not fully optimized to use such data.

Dealing with Mobile Targets

Senior defense officials believe that the fighting in Afghanistan shows that since the Gulf War the United States has made significant advances in addressing the problem of identifying and destroying mobile targets. During the Gulf War, the USAF and USN unsuccessfully targeted Iraq's Scud missiles, flying 1,460 sorties that failed to destroy a single missile battery. In contrast, during the fighting in Afghanistan, the USN has attacked 2,500 mobile targets and claims to have achieved a 65 percent hit rate.

As of June 2002, the USN claimed that aircraft had struck 2,000 mobile targets.[83] Experts attribute this significant achievement to the use of improved precision munitions and communications technology as well as the use UAVs to gather target information. USAF officials also cite the presence of Special Forces personnel, who could more readily identify mobile targets from the ground, as crucial to the success of the air missions over Afghanistan.

The use of satellite-guided smart bombs, which are accurate regardless of weather conditions, along with reliance on the JSTARS, which can track several mobile targets simultaneously, have also contributed to the increased level of success in hitting mobile targets. On the basis of the successful integration of ground forces and air forces in pursuit of mobile targets, it is likely that "Scud hunting" may be a key feature of any future conflict with Iraq.[84]

In Afghanistan, targeting data from the JSTARS were fed directly to F-15E pilots, allowing them to respond quickly and strike a target before its location changed. Although UAVs, such as the Global Hawk, were able to provide imagery of mobile targets, a means to transmit such information directly to USAF and USN pilots has yet to be developed. UAV information is currently transmitted to the CAOC in Saudi Arabia, where analysts determine potential targets and relay specific target coordinates to the battlefield. Military officials describe the CAOC as an essential component that has greatly enhanced U.S. efforts in Afghanistan. As a hub of communications between unmanned and manned aircraft, it has provided commanders with a complete, up-to-date picture of the battlefield.[85]

The first series of technology upgrades, Block 10, has been introduced at Prince Sultan Air Base in Saudi Arabia and includes new networking capabilities for ISR. As a result of the conflict in Afghanistan, the USAF is examining accelerating the introduction of Block 20 technologies that will bring increased speed to the automation of ISR capabilities but may temporarily lead to increased personnel levels while new systems are linked. Efforts are also being made to finalize a vision of Block 30 improvements that will allow reductions in personnel levels at AOCs while providing commanders a "knowledge wall" of battlefield data, including the location of friendly and enemy forces, weapons systems, and mobile targets. Along with the introduction of new systems, however, the USAF must constantly reevaluate its manpower requirements as well as AOC personnel training programs that will need to address technology advances to allow for the most effective training of AOC personnel.[86]

If the USAF and USN are to further increase the percentage of successful hits to mobile targets, it will be necessary to reduce the sensor-to-shooter time between UAVs and fighters by developing direct lines of communication between the unmanned and manned aircraft. Some steps have been taken to address this issue, as evidenced by the

USAF's linking of Predator imagery directly to the cockpit of AC-130 gunships. This, in turn, has allowed the gunship crews to determine the location and features of their target area before reaching it. Much work, however, remains.[87]

The Problem of ISR Asset Density

Afghanistan may have been a small war, but it consumed a very large percentage of total U.S. ISR assets. The United States used at least four photo-reconnaissance-class satellites and two radar-imaging satellites in the operation; experts estimate that Afghanistan and the surrounding area can be photographed roughly every two hours.[88]

CIA director George Tenet instructed the military and intelligence community to rely on high-resolution imagery from private satellite networks to complete more basic tasks such as assembling aerial maps of Afghanistan. The campaign in Afghanistan has been the first time that the U.S. military has relied on private-satellite data. Tenet's directive preserves the use of the limited but more sophisticated and higher-resolution government satellites for specific tasks such as determining precise military targets and assessing the damage from a U.S. or coalition strike against a target.[89]

There were equal limitations in ISR resources at the tactical level. The number of Special Forces teams that could be deployed to provide on-the-ground intelligence and targeting designation was very limited and was probably only a fraction of the number that will be found useful in the future.[90] Many on-the-ground data links, targeting systems, and communications systems provided to Special Forces and rear-area intelligence/targeting analysts lacked the desired range and reliability and can still be greatly improved.[91] Other improvements include the provision of lighter and longer-range laser designators as well as light ATVs and trucks that offer higher mobility and less detectability than systems like the high-mobility multipurpose wheeled vehicle (HMMWV).[92]

ISR and Friendly Fire

Almost all of the assets involved can be improved in terms of range, endurance, sensor suits, computers, software, and secure high-density communications links in order to increase simultaneously the tactical impact of given strikes and their lethality and reduce the risk of friendly fire, civilian casualties, and collateral damage. Although the media have focused largely on collateral damage, putting an end to tragic friendly fire incidents like a May 2002 U.S. air strike on Canadian forces that killed four soldiers during a night exercise is as important as avoiding strikes on civilians.[93]

This May 2002 incident was due more to pilot error and command decisions than to any fault in the ISR system. An F-16 pilot dropped a GBU-12 laser-guided 500-pound bomb on Canadian troops in a night firing exercise. The pilot said he did so because he felt he was under attack although he was flying at 28,000 feet.[94] Nevertheless, a more integrated ISR system might have told the pilot there were friendly forces on the ground. A similar incident in December 2001, when a B-52 dropped a 2,000 pound JDAM that killed three U.S. soldiers and wounded twenty, might also have been avoided.[95]

There have also been many ambiguous cases involving Afghan civilians who may or may not have been taking hostile action or who were near to or mixed with hostile individuals. One example is the incident of July 1, 2002—40 Afghans in a wedding party died when an AC-130 fired in response to what it said was hostile fire, but an after-action ground investigation could find no readily available confirming evidence of such fire. This is only one of the many cases of no clear dividing line between the problem of friendly fire and collateral damage.[96]

It is not clear that minimizing friendly fire has as yet been given the proper priority in U.S. ISR designs and procedures. Certainly technology may be approaching the point where some form of personal identification of friend or foe (IFF) system might be both affordable and detectable by U.S. ISR assets.

The Problem of Decision Time

Some analysts feel that the Afghan conflict shows that reducing decision time is now a critical issue. They feel that changes to the sensor-to-shooter cycle suggest that the find-fix-track-target-attack-assess (FFTTAA) parts of the sensor-to-shooter cycle have improved so much since Desert Storm and Kosovo that U.S. forces now have the ability to find, classify, and put ordinance on targets before the targets can get away. For example, in Desert Storm it took in one particular instance 80 minutes to complete the sensor-to-shooter cycle when identifying and targeting an SA-2 site, but in Afghanistan sensor-to-shooter times decreased on average to just 20 minutes.[97]

Indeed, in Afghanistan it was not these problems that caused U.S. aircraft to miss opportunities to destroy targets. Instead, because of the time it took to make the decision to attack, it was the decision time necessary to get authorization to act that cost opportunities to engage legitimate targets. Analysts feel that examination of the data and lessons learned during the war will show that decision time has become the "long pole in the tent." Shortening the decision segment of the cycle would have a major effect on the future ability of the United States to strike time-sensitive targets and, therefore, improve future combat effectiveness.[98]

The decision-time issue, however, is rooted in the problem of command authorities and the rules of engagement (ROE) as promulgated, interpreted, and acted upon—more specifically the extent to which the decision authority should be delegated to subordinate components and/or operational-tactical levels of command. Afghanistan (like every other conflict) has unique political aspects—the extent and perceptions of collateral damage were very important in the broader context of how the international Muslim community (and others) would react to U.S. operations against a terrorist network that happened to be associated with Muslims.

As a result, ROE were applied that had a significant impact on the length of the decision process and drove the time length of the decision segment far more than any other element (like weapon accuracy) in this part of the cycle. The less precise the guidance provided to the war fighter or the more restrictive the ROE, the longer it takes to complete the decision segment of the cycle. One possible reason is that technical components of the FFTTAA steps in the cycle have received primary attention and resources over the past 10 years and are more optimized from the standpoint of putting ordinance on target; but the technology, systems, and procedures the United States has today do not do as well when it comes to acquiring and disseminating the types of information the person in the loop needs to determine whether the ROE permit attacking the target.

The fighting in Afghanistan was unique in that after the initial stages, a majority of USN aircraft began their missions either without specific targets or had their designated targets changed while in flight. The Navy estimates that roughly 80 percent of the total number of Navy-led air strikes were against time-critical targets identified during a mission. This was in part because of the significant time lag that resulted from having aircraft based far from the battlefield. In many cases, mission briefings occurred up to nine hours before aircraft actually arrived on scene. In the interim, targets and the overall layout of the battlefield often changed, leading to a situation in which the number of in-flight aircraft sometimes outnumbered the number of identified targets. While there is evidence to suggest that technology improvements have enabled the military to become more adept at handling a free-flowing targeting environment, some analysts argue that the military must work to improve its time-critical strike capabilities.[99]

To execute a time-critical strike successfully, an aircraft must be equipped with the necessary munitions. JDAM and other satellite-guided munitions, for example, require more targeting time than a laser-guided munition, in part because a pilot must obtain specific GPS coordinates, check their accuracy, and then input them into a computer before launching a satellite-guided bomb. Making successful use of laser-guided munitions, however, requires that pilots be able to spot and maintain a lock on a target from their aircraft. In many cases, the fighter aircraft on these missions were not equipped with adequate forward-looking infrared sensors (FLIR), making it difficult for pilots to complete this task. Because the pilot and wingman aboard the aircraft do not have the opportunity to study maps of a target given to them in midflight, the need for quality sensors is especially critical to the success of a time-critical strike. Even with accurate sensors and information from AWACS and other surveillance aircraft, pilots indicate they worry whether they are in fact striking the right target.[100]

Availability of FLIR systems contributes to training problems as well. Many officials express concern that the constant rotation of FLIR equipment from carrier to carrier leads to shortcomings in training opportunities. Advances have been made in FLIR technology, and the new AT-FLIR is supposed to provide pilots with an improved picture of the target. Additional enhancement could be made to combat aircraft by connecting them directly to UAVs and by providing pilots with the same real-time video of the target zone that commanders on the ground have. Combined with improvements in communications, these modifications are necessary to increase accuracy in time-critical strike situations. Aircraft had the luxury of flying over a target area multiple times in Afghanistan before they dropped their munitions, in part because the enemy lacked the weapons technology to pose a threat to U.S. aircraft. In future conflicts, U.S. aircraft may not have this luxury, and quick identification and destruction of a target will become vital.[101]

If these conclusions are supported by the facts and data being extracted from the official review of the lessons of Afghanistan, one of the transformational implications of the war is that improving the decision segment of the sensor-to-shooter cycle can have transformational effects at little or no cost. It may also be possible to determine which categories of hardware, systems, and procedures still need to be developed or improved to contribute information and data to facilitate the ROE process or remove procedural impediments to achieving the objectives of the ROE without missing opportunities to engage legitimate targets.[102]

Problems of Targeting, Intelligence, and Battle Damage Assessment

Technology is only part of the challenge. During the Gulf War, Desert Fox, and again in Afghanistan, the United States has faced several major problems in using its strike power effectively, problems that will not be solved with better sensors and command, control, communications, computers, and information (C⁴I) systems. The problems in targeting terrorist and asymmetric forces have already been touched upon, as have the related problems of estimating collateral damage and civilian casualties.

These problems are almost certain to be just as serious in future conflicts, regardless of type. Most Middle Eastern wars will not be mud-hut conflicts, and the United States may well face larger-scale conventional contingencies in which a power—like Iraq—chooses to fight inside cities and urban areas rather than in the open desert. The United States may also have to strike at dispersed CBRN facilities and forces. Furthermore, the United States may find that the efforts of factions to use or mislead the U.S. conduct of strike operations—as occurred in Afghanistan—can be a problem in a nation like Iraq as well.

The United States already makes a major effort to avoid collateral damage in its air strikes, and the United States applies highly demanding ROE in Afghanistan:

- First, it takes account of malfunctions and errors. Malfunctions and errors can occur with weapons, which is why classified planning data have been created to predict such problems and why the United States follows procedures—run-in restrictions, target acquisition/lock ROE, abort criteria, and preanalysis planning of weapon/target match—to try to mitigate such incidents.

- Second, it explicitly estimates probable collateral damage to surrounding people and structures as a potential result of hitting the correct target. The preanalysis considers specific munitions effects in the initial munitions selection. Depending on the potential expected collateral damage, different modeling tools are available to determine the best kill–minimum damage ratio (for example, a JWAC level-four analysis is conducted if necessary). Even given the potential for type-two collateral damage, a conscious command decision is often made (with lawyers involved) to determine if the desired military effect is proportional to the level of expected collateral damage.

The U.S. ability to locate some kinds of targets is far better than its ability to characterize them, judge their importance, and assess the level of damage it did to their functional capabilities after it strikes them. The United States did not demonstrate during the Gulf War,

Desert Fox, and in Afghanistan that it had a valid doctrine for striking at leadership, infrastructure, and civilian C⁴I, lines of communication, and other rear-area strategic targets. It essentially guessed at their importance and bombed for effect.

Gen. Tommy Franks gave testimony to the Senate Armed Services Committee that while the United States needed an average of 10 aircraft to take out a target in Desert Storm, a single aircraft could often take out two targets during the fighting in Afghanistan.[103] It seems almost certain, however, that these figures will ultimately prove to be just as unrealistic as the initial battle damage and effectiveness claims made in the Gulf War, Desert Fox, and Kosovo.

The U.S. military services and the intelligence community simply do not have a credible battle damage assessment capability. They use an ever-changing set of rules that transforms vague and inadequate damage indicators into detailed estimates by category and type. These rules and methods have only the crudest of analytic controls and cannot survive simple review methods like blind testing. They rely heavily on imagery that cannot look inside buildings and shelters, often cannot tell whether a weapon was inactive or had already been damaged by fire, and is essentially worthless in estimating infantry and human casualties. The interpreters also constantly change and receive limited training with few controls and little validation. Battle damage assessment is an art form with far too few artists.

The U.S. ability to characterize sheltered and closed-in targets remains weak, as does its ability to assess and strike at hardened targets. This remains a major problem in the case of nations, like Iraq and Iran, that make extensive use of such facilities, but it is important to note that U.S. sensors and teams on the ground never succeeded in characterizing many much simpler Taliban and Al Qaeda facilities— caves, for example. The Navy SEAL team that explored the cave complex at Zhawar Kili in February had no idea that it would turn out to be the largest complex yet uncovered. The team had to physically enter the area to determine that U.S. air strikes on the facility had had little or no effect, and the team left large stocks of supplies intact.[104]

The United States has a better ability to assess physical damage to surface buildings but limited ability to assess damage to their contents. Its ability to assess functional damage to complex systems, like land-based air defense systems, and the resulting degree of degradation in the systems' operational capabilities is also generally weak. The United States had major problems in these areas during the Gulf War, Kosovo, and the 10 years of strikes against the Iraqi air defense system. The United States had—and still has—major problems locating key targets like the leadership of hostile powers and the facilities and forces related to weapons of mass destruction.

The Middle East presents particularly serious challenges in terms of proliferation. The United States and its allies face ongoing problems in terms of proliferation in Iran, Iraq, and Syria and the possible acquisition of such weapons by terrorist forces. More broadly, the ability to perform reliable battle damage assessment—even in dealing with conventional military targets like armor, major weapons, depots, and infantry—remains a weak link in the U.S. ability to close the loop.

In short, Afghanistan is yet another warning that the ability to close the loop and the many other potential advantages of the RMA require far better strategic assessment and intelligence capabilities to determine the nature and importance of targets, better ways to assess the strategic impact of the targets and the impact of striking them, and an honest admission by the U.S. military services and intelligence community that its battle damage assessment methods are crude and inadequate if not intellectually dishonest.

THE PROBLEM OF INTELLIGENCE

Afghanistan teaches broader lessons regarding intelligence. Afghanistan again showed the need to maintain a large cadre with language and area skills to deal with the need for area expertise, to conduct coalition warfare, to support ground and air operations, and to handle the complexities of targeting and battle damage assessment. The fact that the United States was concentrated on China in the spring of 2001 but was concentrated on Afghanistan and some 67 other countries after September 11 shows that developing a suitable pool of field and analysis capabilities cannot be tied to predictions about future threats and scenarios.

Improving Intelligence Capabilities

HUMINT is one important aspect of building up suitable capabilities, but its importance and value have often been exaggerated. It takes an average of two years to recruit, validate, and train a foreign source. The British found in dealing with Northern Ireland that it often took seven years to go farther and penetrate a tightly organized network in some element of the IRA. U.S. military officials did find human intelligence to be extremely helpful in making the decision to design and initiate the attack on Al Qaeda and Taliban forces in the Shah-i-Kot valley, but they also emphasized the importance of combining that information from HUMINT with information from other sources in an attempt to develop the most accurate picture of the battlefield situation.[105]

Afghanistan has been yet another demonstration that most human sources are unreliable or have only limited access to the collection target. Their information has often been of only limited value and credibility unless it can be cross-correlated by an analyst using other intelligence sources. In short, HUMINT can help in some areas; but it normally will not be a solution to any major problem in technical intelligence collection, and it has little or negative value without major improvements in analysis and the ability to focus and fuse all-source intelligence collection.

Similarly, data mining can automate some aspects of intelligence collection and can enable the intelligence community to make far better use of unclassified media and other sources. It can also help recognize patterns in terms of indications and warning. Data mining, however, is not a substitute for analysis and for large analytic staffs. At present, data mining also makes a far better impression on the contractors and data systems experts who promote it than it makes on the intelligence analysts and military personnel who use it. To be of real help and to not simply automate the problem of translating collection into analysis, data mining must be highly adaptable, easy to use, and constantly tailored by an experienced analyst to a specific need.

There is also a major difference between good collection and analysis and effective support of military operations. Afghanistan is also yet another demonstration that virtually all low-intensity and asymmetric wars require both intelligence and military personnel on the ground to support coalition operations, directly support targeting, and gain information in real time that can support operations. The United States was fortunate that it had some recent regional Special Forces experience in Afghanistan, but it possessed only a very limited pool of appropriate military and CIA operations personnel and almost certainly would have done better with more.

Dispersed warfare adds to the problem, particularly in friendly states. Since Operation Anaconda, intelligence operatives from the FBI have been working closely with U.S. military personnel hunting in Pakistan for Al Qaeda fighters. This new relationship is said to be closer than the previous relationships between military and intelligence services. FBI agents stationed in cities across Pakistan work to gather information on the whereabouts of suspected Al Qaeda and Taliban fighters and then relay that information to U.S. Special Forces and Pakistani security forces who then decide whether to pursue the leads. Aware of local sensitivities, FBI agents have been careful to keep their presence muted, and they rarely, if ever, accompany their Pakistani counterparts on raids.[106]

U.S. officials credit the new level of communication between the military and intelligence community as being responsible for the raid that led to the capture of Abu Zubaydah, believed to be Al Qaeda's field commander. The FBI has also assisted Pakistani security agents in successfully apprehending more than 70 suspected Islamic militants residing in major Pakistani cities. Following a failed raid at a *madrasa,* however, residents in the city of Miram Shah staged a protest against the FBI's presence and involvement in such raids. The key to continued success, therefore, will be the FBI's ability to maintain a low profile yet still assist in efforts to capture militants.[107]

In short, improved intelligence and operations require improvements in all five areas: technical collection, processing and fusion, HUMINT, SIGINT, and operations. Improving any given area and particularly ignoring analysis are not lessons of the war in Afghanistan and would make for an almost certain recipe for failure.

Indications and Warning

Finally, it seems highly doubtful that improvements in intelligence will succeed in doing a much better job of guaranteeing indications and warnings than the United States did before September 11, 2001. It is important that the United States had long seen Al Qaeda as an enemy and had prevented several previous attacks. September 11 came because Al Qaeda changed its methods, had an unusually expert group of attackers, and was lucky. It seems likely that future attackers will innovate and some will be highly professional and lucky.

Since the beginning of the Cold War, the United States has conducted various postcrises indications-and-warning studies. Some produced scapegoats, and some caused significant improvements to be made in indications-and-warning capabilities. In general, however, indications-and-warning analysis has only kept pace with the evolution of threat techniques. The chance that any post-Afghanistan improvements in indications and warning will be enough to prevent the success of future attacks is probably close to zero.

NOTES

[1] *Inside the Air Force,* July 12, 2002, p. 1.

[2] *San Diego Union-Tribune,* June 24, 2002.

[3] *Washington Post,* June 24, 2002, p. 13

[4] *Defense News,* May 6, 2002, p. 34.

[5] *Defense News,* May 20, 2002, p. 32.

[6] For a particularly good summary of the fighting, see Richard T. Cooper, "The Untold War," *Los Angeles Times,* March 24, 2002; Cincinnatus, "Operation Anaconda," *Soldier of Fortune,* www.sofmag.com; and Bradley Graham, "Bravery and Breakdowns in a Ridgetop Battle, May 24, 2002, p. A-1; and "A Wintry Ordeal at 10,000 Feet," *Washington Post,* May 25, 2002, p. A-1. Also see Associated Press, March 6, 2002; *Washington Post,* March 6, 2002, p. 1; March 13, 2002, p. 19; March 14, 2002, p. 1; May 24, 2002, A-1; *Asia Pacific Defense Reporter,* May 2002, pp. 34–36; *London Daily Telegraph,* March 5, 2002; *Los Angeles Times,* March 11, 2002.

[7] *Washington Post,* May 24, 2002, A-1; *Asia Pacific Defense Reporter,* May 2002, pp. 34–36; *London Times,* June 18, 2002.

[8] *Boston Globe,* March 9, 2002, p. D-2.

[9] *Washington Post,* March 4, 2002, p. A-1.

[10] *Boston Globe,* March 9, 2002, p. D-2.

[11] *Washington Post,* May 24, 2002, p. A-1.

[12] Ibid.

[13] *Asia Pacific Defense Reporter,* May 2002, pp. 34–36; *Soldier of Fortune,* June 2002.

[14] *Washington Times,* March 12, 2002, p. 3.

[15] *London Telegraph,* March 5, 2002.

[16] *Asia Pacific Defense Reporter,* May 2002, pp. 34–36.

[17] Ibid.

[18] *Boston Globe,* March 9, 2002, p. D-2.

[19] *Asia Pacific Defense Reporter,* May 2002, pp. 34–36.

[20] *London Times,* March 4, 2002; *Asia Pacific Defense Reporter,* May 2002, pp. 34–36.

[21] *London Times,* March 4, 2002.

[22] *Defense News,* July 22–28, 2002, p. 38; see also "Emerging Lessons, Insights, and Observations: Operation Enduring Freedom," prepared by the Center for Army Lessons Learned, Fort Leavenworth, Kansas; *Washington Post,* April 28, 2002, p. 16.

[23] *Defense News,* July 22–28, 2002, p. 38; see also "Emerging Lessons, Insights, and Observations: Operation Enduring Freedom"; *Washington Post,* April 28, 2002, p. 16.

[24] Ibid.

[25] *Washington Post,* June 3, 2002, p. 13.

[26] Bloomberg News Service, May 21, 2002; *Army Times,* March 6, 2002.

[27] *Army Times,* May 20, 2002, p. 9.

[28] *Defense News,* July 22–28, 2002, p. 38; see also "Emerging Lessons, Insights, and Observations: Operation Enduring Freedom"; Bloomberg News Service, May 21, 2002.

[29] *Defense News,* June 17, 2002, p. 1.

[30] *Defense News,* July 15–21, 2002, p. 40.

[31] Ibid.

[32] Ibid.

[33] *Washington Post,* March 10, 2002, p. A-26.

[34] *Defense News,* May 13, 2002.

[35] *Defense Week,* December 17, 2002, p. 2.

[36] For excellent reporting on this issues, see Craig Covault, "US Military Wants Sweeping Satcom Changes," *Aviation Week & Space Technology,* January 21, 2002, p. 27.

[37] Ibid.

[38] *Wall Street Journal,* April 10, 2002.

[39] *Washington Post,* May 22, 2002, p. 26.

[40] See washingtonpost.com, June 3, 2002, p. A-l.

[41] *New York Times,* February 4, 2002.

[42] *Defense News,* July 22–28, 2002, p. 38; see also "Emerging Lessons, Insights, and Observations: Operation Enduring Freedom."

[43] *Defense Week,* April 1, 2002, p. 8.

[44] *Asia Pacific Defense Reporter,* May 2002, pp. 34–36.

[45] Gen. Tommy Franks's testimony to the Senate Armed Services Committee on February 7, 2002; Bryan Bender, Kim Burger, and Andrew Koch, "Afghanistan: First Lessons," *Jane's Defense Weekly,* December 19, 2001, p. 20; *New York Times,* February 8, 2002, p. A-14; *Philadelphia Inquirer,* February 12, 2002, p. 1.

[46] *New York Times,* June 25, 2002.

[47] For a more detailed assessment of these points and why the air environment in Afghanistan may not be relevant to fighting against countries like Iran, Iraq, and North Korea, see the presentation of Gen. Hal Hornburg, commander of the Air Combat Command, and Gen. Gregory Martin, commander of USAFE, before the Air Force Association Conference in Orlando, Florida, as reported in Bloomburg.com, February 20, 2002; see also www.afa.org/magazine/April2002/0402Orl.pdf.

[48] *Norfolk Virginian-Pilot,* July 12, 2002.

[49] *USA Today,* April 30, 2002; *Jane's Defense Weekly,* December 5, 2001, p. 3; *Los Angeles Times,* December 11, 2001; Time.com, April 27, 2002.

[50] *Defense Daily,* March 25, 2002, p. 48; July 3, 2002, p. 1; *Wall Street Journal,* May 3, 2002.

[51] *Defense Daily,* July 3, 2002, p.1; *Aviation Week & Space Technology,* April 29, 2002, p. 55.

[52] *Jane's Defense Weekly,* January 16, 2002, p. 3; *Washington Times,* April 2, 2002, p. 5.

[53] *Defense Daily,* July 9, 2002, p. 3.

[54] *Air Force News,* May 29, 2002.

[55] This list is provided by CENTCOM. Also see *Jane's Defense Weekly,* March 13, 2002, pp. 4, 21.

[56] *Washington Times,* July 11, 2002, p. 15.

[57] *Washington Post,* June 21, 2002, p. 19.

[58] *Baltimore Sun,* July 10, 2002.

[59] For a good preliminary analysis of these lessons of war, see Bryan Bender, Kim Burger, and Andrew Koch, "Afghanistan: First Lessons," *Jane's Defense Weekly,* December 19, 2001, pp. 18–21.

[60] *Aerospace Daily,* February 20, 2002; Gen. Tommy Franks's testimony to the Senate Armed Services Committee on February 7, 2002.

[61] See Sandra I. Erwin, "Naval aviation: lessons from war; Enduring Freedom reinforces need for new targeting pods, radar, data links," *National Defense* (publication of National Defense Industrial Association), June 1, 2002, p. 16.

[62] *Aerospace Daily,* February 20, 2002; Gen. Tommy Franks's testimony to the Senate Armed Services Committee on February 7, 2002.

[63] ABC News background brief and *Defense Daily,* April 10, 2002, p. 7.

[64] For a good discussion of the operational strengths and weaknesses of current systems, see Christopher J. Bowie, "Destroying Mobile Ground Targets in an Anti-Access Environment," Northrop Grumman Analysis Center Paper, Washington, D.C., December 2001, www.capitol.northgrum.com/files/mobile_ground_targets.pdf.

[65] *Defense News,* January 3, 2002, p. 1.

[66] *Defense News,* March 25, 2002, p. 8

[67] James G. Roche, "Transforming the Air Force," *Joint Forces Quarterly,* Autumn/Winter 2001–2002, pp. 9–12; *Defense News,* January 3, 2002, p. 1.

[68] *Los Angeles Times,* July 15, 2002.

[69] For more details, see *Defense News,* April 22, 2002, p. 28; March 25, 2002, p. 8.

[70] Joseph N. Mait and Jon G. Grossman, "Relevancy and Risk: The U.S. Army and Future Combat Systems," *Defense Horizons,* Center for Technology and National Security Policy, National Defense University, May 2002, p. 4, www.ndu.edu/inss/DefHor/DH13/DH13.pdf.

[71] See Lt. Col. Merrick Krause, "How to Project Power: Asset Integration, Not Platforms, Get Results," *Defense News,* June 3, 2002, p. 19.

[72] Mait and Grossman, "Relevancy and Risk," p. 4; *Defense Weekly,* daily update, July 3, 2002.

[73] *Wall Street Journal,* April 10, 2002.

[74] Ibid.

[75] *Defense News,* February 11, 2002, p. 3; *USA Today,* March 11, 2002, p. 3B.

[76] *Boston Globe,* February 6, 2002, p. 10; *Jane's Defense Weekly,* January 2, 2002, p. 6.

[77] *Washington Post,* July 13, 2002, p. 11.

[78] *Washington Post,* March 26, 2002, A-1.

[79] Ibid.

[80] Ibid.

[81] *Defense News,* June 10, 2002, p. 20.

[82] *Defense News,* May 6, 2002, p. 6.

[83] *Defense Daily,* July 9, 2002, p. 3.

[84] *Washington Post,* July 5, 2002, p. 14.

[85] Ibid.; *Air Force News,* May 29, 2002; *Aviation Week & Space Technology,* March 11, 2002, p. 24.

[86] *Inside the Air Force,* July 5, 2002, p. 1.

[87] *Washington Post,* July 5, 2002, p. 14; *Air Force News,* May 29, 2002.

[88] *Jane's Defense Weekly,* October 17, 2001, p. 6.

[89] *New York Times,* June 26, 2002.

[90] Dana Priest, "In War, Mud Huts and Hard Calls," *Washington Post,* February 20, 2002, pp. A-1, A-8.

[91] *Defense News,* February 11–17, 2002, p. 8.

[92] Ibid.

[93] *Ottawa Citizen,* June 26, 2002, p. 12.

[94] *New York Times,* June 19, 2002; *Washington Post,* June 19, 2002, p. 22.

[95] *International Herald Tribune,* December 7, 2001; *Christian Science Monitor,* December 7, 2001.

[96] Jim Garamone, "Operations Continue in Eastern Afghanistan," American Forces Information Service, July 18, 2002, www.defense link.mil/news/Jul2002/n07182002_200207183.html.

[97] Mait and Grossman, "Relevancy and Risk," p. 4.

[98] For an interesting Israeli perspective on these issues, see Avi Kober, "Reflections on Battlefield Decision and Low Intensity Conflict," Bar-Ilan University, BESA Center for Strategic Studies, May 2002.

[99] Erwin, "Naval aviation"; *Aviation Week & Space Technology,* April 29, 2002, p. 55.

[100] Erwin, "Naval aviation."

[101] Ibid.

[102] Ibid.

[103] *Aerospace Daily,* February 20, 2002; Gen. Tommy Franks's testimony to the Senate Armed Services on February 7, 2002.

[104] *Washington Post,* February 16, 2002, p. A-27.

[105] *Defense Week,* April 1, 2002, p. 8.

[106] *New York Times,* July 14, 2002, p. A-1.

[107] Ibid.

CHAPTER SIX

THE CHALLENGE OF
FORCE TRANSFORMATION

There is no easy way to separate the reaction of the Department of Defense to the lessons of Afghanistan from its broader force transformation efforts that began early in the Bush administration but had much of their genesis more than a decade ago in the RMA. The most recent Quadrennial Defense Review (QDR) was issued in the late fall of 2001, before there had been time to react to the course of the fighting in Afghanistan. The QDR set six major goals for force transformation: protect the U.S. homeland and critical bases of operation; deny enemies sanctuary; project and sustain power in access-denied areas; leverage information technology; improve and protect information operations; and enhance space operations. Of these goals, some have application to the lessons of Afghanistan. Furthermore, planning and budgeting documents issued since that time reflect both the Defense Department's view of the initial lessons of Afghanistan and its conclusion that the U.S. experience in fighting terrorism has validated many of the conclusions of its earlier force transformation studies.

THE FORCE TRANSFORMATION PDM

Although no unclassified version is available and the plans for many aspects of the U.S. force transformation effort are not yet complete, press reports indicate that U.S. Program Decision Memorandum 4, the so-called Transformation PDM, called for the following:[1]

- Improve satellite communications at an approximate cost of $2 billion;

- Accelerate unmanned combat vehicle programs and examine new programs that will supplement or replace manned combat aircraft:

  - Procure more RQ-1 Predators with the ability to fire air-to-ground (AGM-114) Hellfire missiles; and
  - Examine the option of arming the Predators with smaller 250 to 500-pound versions of the JDAM;

- Modify and improve the GPS satellites for security and survivability;

- Procure much larger numbers of RQ-1 Predator, RQ-4A Global Hawk, and other UAV intelligence and targeting systems, including possible conversions to UAVs of retired manned aircraft or older target drones like the BQM-145, BQM-34S, and MQM-34D;[2]

- Improve UAV endurance, payload capability, sensors, downlinks, survivability, and launch/recovery systems, including their electro-optical, infrared, and synthetic aperture radar sensors (approximately 20 of the 68 Predators delivered to date have been lost, largely to operator error or enemy fire); add UAVs to future maritime patrol aircraft;[3]

- Improve space-based radars and imagery systems;

- Procure and improve Tomahawk cruise missile systems;

- Convert at least four more C-130s into gunships, and improve AC-130 special operations combat aircraft and other Special Forces variants of the C-130, including countermeasures for air defense; improve video and infrared targeting and surveillance systems and fire-control capability, and refine the data-link systems between the AC-130 and Predator/Global Hawks that were rushed into deployment during the Afghan War;[4]

- Procure and improve portable and theater-deployable intelligence and targeting systems as well as rear echelon and national capabilities;

- Improve communications, secure data links, displays, weapons dispensers, and precision weapons to make real-time targeting and restrike capabilities more effective;

- Accelerate the airborne laser theater missile defense system;

- Spend $63 million for upgrade of NORAD computers and radars;

- Accelerate hard-target and underground-facility penetration weapons to replace or enhance the GBU-28 5,000-pound bunker-buster bombs and AGM-130s used to attack hard and deeply buried targets during the Afghan War; examine ways to add hard-target kill capabilities to cruise missiles (unconfirmed reports indicate that one such missile, the AGM-86D, was used during the Afghan fighting); other options include a hard-target-defeat thermobaric weapon, the FMU-157 hard-target smart fuze, and the BLU-116B advanced unitary penetrator warhead;[5] and

- Accelerate programs to develop unattended ground sensors and long-loiter collection platforms to characterize and monitor activities in facilities, and develop remote sensors for the penetration of caves and sheltered facilities.

Almost every item on this list has some relation to the U.S. experience in Afghanistan and to some extent responds to the lessons of either Afghanistan or the broader war on terrorism.

DEFENSE PLANNING GUIDANCE AND FUTURE MILITARY STRATEGY

The defense planning guidance (DPG) for 2004–2009, issued in May 2002, also reflects the lessons that are being learned from the campaign in Afghanistan. Reflecting the Bush administration's shift toward a military doctrine of preemptive action against possible enemies, the DPG calls for accelerating force transformation efforts by developing and fielding a new generation of weapons that relies on advanced technology to enhance its effectiveness. Secretary Rumsfeld contends that by developing the weapons systems and forces needed to carry out preemptive action, the United States will create a new form of forward deterrence that will make enemies think twice about striking the United States. Under the DPG, all branches of the military are ordered to develop capabilities necessary to execute rapid preemptive strikes against enemies.[6]

Under the guidelines established by the DPG, military spending will be focused on addressing five specific needs: countering and combating terrorism and the proliferation of weapons of mass destruction (WMD), enhancing ISR capabilities, developing new methods of protecting against and waging cyber warfare, enhancing space-based military capabilities, and further developing precision air-strike capabilities. Specifically, the DPG calls for the development of a squadron of unmanned fighter jets by 2012, as well as the development by 2009 of a hypersonic missile that can travel 600 nautical miles in 15 minutes and destroy mobile targets before the enemy can reposition them.[7]

During the fighting in Afghanistan, the United States has dropped a significant number of precision munitions. The DPG outlines a future high-volume precision strike capability characterized by the use of a large number of smaller, more accurate precision munitions dropped on an enemy from a fleet of unmanned aircraft. Combined with other advances in military technology, these technologies are designed to enhance and further the military's capability to rapidly strike an enemy practically anywhere in the world.[8]

As a result of fighting in Afghanistan in which the United States frequently targeted Al Qaeda cave complexes and bunkers, the DPG outlines the need to develop the ability to use laser and microwave-powered weapons to conduct high-volume precision strikes against an enemy. The DPG also acknowledges the need for development of a nuclear bunker-busting bomb that will destroy enemy compounds and supplies of WMD hidden far beneath the ground in hardened bunkers. The Department of Defense estimates that there are some 10,000 hard and deeply buried targets (HDBTs) in the world (most are 20 meters or less underground, however), that some 1,000 have critical strategic value, and that their number will increase steadily as improved tunneling equipment becomes available.

Beyond advanced weapons capabilities, the DPG argues that if a doctrine of preemptive strikes is to be effective, new efforts must be made to improve intelligence capabilities, enabling the United States to both become aware of a future threat and more accurately determine and target the strength and location of enemy. Based on the experience in Afghanistan, the DPG also calls for improving the execution of and training for joint operations.[9]

Shapers of the new DPG cite the successful use of Special Forces and precision air support in Afghanistan as reason to further develop lighter, more stealth capabilities. The risk remains, however, that in certain military situations, rapid-response lightweight forces may not be appropriate. With the fighting continuing in Afghanistan, military planners must be careful not to make blanket generalizations based on what has so far been a unique war. To do so will risk creating gaps in U.S. military and force capabilities. Also, in its rush to embrace the military techniques of Afghanistan, the DPG continues to ignore the political, economic, and social realities that remain significant problems and roadblocks on the way to the successful completion of any military operation.[10]

Other Defense Department studies are under way, focusing specifically on developing joint headquarters, the force capability needed to enact new strategies, and the C^{4}ISR technologies needed to support the new strategy.[11]

AFGHANISTAN AND THE FORCE TRANSFORMATION IMPACT OF THE FY 2003 BUDGET

The president's FY 2003 budget request sets forth a list of additional force transformation efforts, including:

- Convert four Trident submarines to cruise missile carriers; the budget also seeks to capitalize on U.S. asymmetric advantages in the development of new classes of satellites—including a space-based radar—and the improvement of existing capabilities and hardening them against attack;

- Initiate development of the DD(X) surface warfare ship, a test bed for future Navy systems; plans are to insert and test new stealth and propulsion technologies in the DD(X) and also test new manning programs; the budget request is for $961 million for this effort;

- Spend $1 billion on the procurement and research of UAVs; the Defense Department wants to spend $154.1 million to buy and arm 22 USAF Predator UAVs in fiscal 2003; the Air Force has also allocated $170.8 million for three Global Hawk UAVs; there is another $100.7 million set aside to buy 12 Army Shadow UAVs;

- Buy 70 more Global Hawks and associated equipment at a cost of $1.55 billion for the USAF and buy 28 for the USN, which the Navy will deploy in seven systems, each with four aircraft and support elements;[12]

- Accelerate funding of Global Hawk research and the Navy's Fire Scout UAV (According to the Pentagon, "these UCAVs are not just UAVs with weapons added…they are combat airplanes built from the ground up, just without pilots"); the request also accelerates research in UCAVs; and increases funding for unmanned underwater vehicles as well as the Defense Advanced Research Projects Agency (DARPA) future UCAV program, with a deployment goal of 2015 for the DARPA UCAV;

- Transform the old strategic nuclear triad—land-based intercontinental ballistic missiles (ICBMs), manned aircraft, and submarine-launched ballistic missiles. President Bush has announced plans to reduce offensive nuclear warheads from 6,000 to between 1,700 and 2,200. The new triad is the scaled-down nuclear deterrent, a more deadly and responsive conventional deterrent, and missile defense;

- Budget for procurement approximately $72 billion, with $13.8 billion for the Army, $24.9 billion for the Navy/Marine Corps, $27.3 billion for the Air Force, and $2.8 billion for Department of Defense–wide buys. There is also $3.2 billion in the defense emergency response fund;

- Increase the budget for research, development, testing, and evaluation to $53.9 billion in FY 2003, up from $48.4 billion a year earlier. This would allow continued development of the joint strike fighter (JSF) and accelerate special operations capability. It also funds the restructured V-22 Osprey program;

- Increase science and technology funding by $1 billion to $9.9 billion, or 2.7 percent of the Department of Defense budget top line. The money would fund USA research in future combat systems (FCSs), medical technology, and other basic research. USN funds would go to mine warfare and mine countermeasures, undersea systems, and basic research. The USAF would look at directed energy, aircraft propulsion, and uses of space;

- Cancel older programs out of line with the transformation strategy, and shift almost $10 billion to other projects. Cancelled projects include the Navy DD-21 destroyer and theater area missile defense programs, the Air Force Peacekeeper missile program, and 18 Army legacy programs. The services will retire some older systems faster, such as older F-14 Tomcats, Vietnam-era UH-1 helicopters, and the Navy's Spruance destroyer class;

- Provide $707 million for the Army's FCS. In addition, the Army would buy 332 interim armored vehicles and 5,631 M-16 rifles; the request budgets $910.2 million for continued development of the RAH-66 Comanche helicopter;

- Fund two DDG-51 Arleigh Burke–class destroyers, a Virginia-class attack submarine, an LPD-17 amphibious transport dock ship, and a Lewis and Clark–class auxiliary dry cargo ship; the Navy would also buy 15 MH-60S helicopters, five E-2C Hawkeye aircraft, and 44 F/A-18E/F Hornet fighters and will also continue with the EA-6B Prowler electronic surveillance and control craft modernization program;

- Fund 12 more C-17 airlifters, one E-8C JSTARS aircraft, and 23 F-22 Raptor fighters; the budget also funds modernization programs for the B-2 Spirit bomber, the F-16 fighter-bomber, and the F-15E multimission fighter.

About half of these force transformation activities have some direct relation to the U.S. experience in Afghanistan although the reason behind including them in the budget request was usually to deal with U.S. global requirements and had little to do with Afghanistan per se. As part of its effort to develop a coherent approach to force transformation, however, the United States now faces the practical problem of shaping these programs to reflect fully the lessons of Afghanistan, not only to redefine missions and war plans but also to ensure that force transformation does not ignore the war's lessons regarding coalition warfare, interoperability, basing and forward-presence requirements, and power projection.

Also as part of the FY 2003 budget, the Bush administration called for the creation of a $19.46 billion war reserve called the defense emergency response fund. Half the reserve total—$10 billion—was not designated for specific uses until July 2002, when the administration sent an amendment to the 2003 defense bill to Congress designating $5.57 billion for follow-on operations including maintenance and repair costs for equipment currently deployed and in preparation to be deployed as well as the cost of maintaining camps, airfields, and staging areas currently in use or in development for use in the war. Another $1.88 billion is for replenishment of the supply of precision guided and conventional munitions, including Hellfire missiles, as well as other bombs needed for continued operations.[13]

In preparing its FY 2004 budget request, the Defense Department is said once again to be evaluating cutting force sizes in an effort to increase the amount of funds available for development of a new generation of weapons systems that it sees as central to transforming the armed forces. Personnel costs totaled roughly 25 percent of the department's FY 2003 budget and exceeded the amount of money spent on the development and purchase of weapons. Media reports differ as to the expected outcome of an internal personnel study being carried out by the Defense Department; some sources indicate that the department is examining cutting one Army division consisting of 20,000–25,000 soldiers as well as 22,000 Navy personnel, 40,000 USAF personnel, and between 2,000 and 5,000 Marines. However, the head of the project, David S. C. Chu, the under secretary of defense for personnel and readiness, has denied this, stating that reports of troop cuts are "a misperception" of his work and that no troop cuts are currently planned. Observers indicate that while specific personnel cuts may not be called for, it is likely that several ongoing studies will reexamine efforts to reduce headquarters staffing, reduce the use of active-duty personnel for certain tasks that do not require their expertise, and determine whether certain services should discontinue groups of specialists and retrain them to perform other tasks.[14]

Whatever the outcome in terms of personnel cuts and retraining, reports indicate a determined effort to press forward with transformation plans that rely on advanced technology and weapons systems and increased automation to perform tasks previously requiring personnel. Some officials and politicians, however, remain concerned that cutting force size in the midst of an ongoing conflict could stretch the military too thin, especially given the demands that current and future peacekeeping missions and efforts to defeat Al Qaeda may place on U.S. forces.[15]

OTHER ADVANCES IN TACTICS AND TECHNOLOGY

The United States is conducting efforts relating to tactics and technology in a number of other areas; some relate to the Afghan War although it is impossible to describe most as direct results of the lessons of the Afghan conflict:[16]

- Pursue a broad goal of tightening the delay to no more than 10 minutes between real-time intelligence gathering and targeting at the shooter platform;
- Develop as part of the FCS a high-speed data network, integrated both vertically and horizontally, that is difficult to detect and intercept and that will provide secure command, control, and communications;[17]

- Improve relevant central planning and data transfer facilities like the American Joint Analysis Center at RAF Molesworth in Cambridgeshire, England, and ensure that the United States does not become overdependent on regional facilities like the CAOC in Saudi Arabia;[18]

- Decrease over the next 10–20 years by 90 percent the total manpower needed to run AOCs such as the CAOC in Saudi Arabia;

- Accelerate the development of systems to detect and characterize biological and chemical weapons and attacks; one particularly promising area for targeting and for Middle Eastern operations is the use of unattended ground sensors to provide capabilities that can monitor and characterize activity in various complexes and buildings and, possibly, in underground facilities;

- Accelerate the development of sea-based wide-area missile defenses and the selection of a suitable replacement to the E-6B electronic warfare aircraft as part of a joint airborne electronics attack program;

- Develop and/or buy small-diameter bombs, cockpit-selectable fusing options, cockpit-selectable "yield" for conventional weapons, and dual-mode seekers (for example, GPS and laser);

- Reexamine the value of weapons like the BLU-82 15,000-pound GSX jellied slurry bomb in terms of hard-target kill and psychological impact, and/or reweaponize fuel-air explosive weapons like the BLU-72;

- Upgrade the communications, display, and munitions systems on B-52 and other U.S. bombers and U.S. strike fighters to improve their ability to retarget in midflight as well as retarget and restrike during the same mission;

- Improve some relevant subsystems on the RC-135V Rivet Joint signals intelligence aircraft and the U-2;[19]

- Improve the J-8 JSTARS targeting software;[20]

- Develop advanced targeting pods for existing aircraft and built-in systems for the JSF, with third-generation forward-looking radar sensors and charge-coupled imagers capable of identifying individual weapons at a distance;

- Increase dissemination of electronic and intermediate-range (IR) intelligence systems and other surveillance platforms on various existing airborne platforms such as tankers;

- Replenish stocks of the GPS-guided JDAMs—the $14,000 kit used to convert regular bombs into smart weapons. By December 2001, approximately 4,600 JDAMs were used out of a total inventory of 10,000. This is roughly 38 percent of the 12,000 weapons used as of that date;[21]

- Enhance use of the WCMD that was used in the Afghan War to dispense more accurately such combined-effects munitions as the CBU-130 (a weapon with some 202 BLU-97/B cluster bombs);

- Complete development of the SFW with a smart IR homing capability for antiarmor and vehicle use, and develop improved submunitions with a fail-safe option to prevent them from remaining live for extended periods;[22]

- Deploy a dedicated multisensor command-and-control aircraft (MC²A) by 2009 to support advanced closed-loop missions, including ones by stealth aircraft like the F-22 and B-2A;[23]

- Improve three-dimensional mapping and imagery to improve the accuracy of GPS-guided weapons and determine the proper angle of attack;[24]

- Begin development of an advanced, next-generation manned or unmanned bomber that is capable of surviving extremely advanced developmental surface-to-air defenses like the Russian S-400 Triumf (SA-20);

- Revise the defense communications satellite and Milstar program to handle far greater communications densities, integrate information systems, standardize on one set of terminals, and downlink communication systems with different echelons of access and security;[25] add Lasercom data and increase support to small, scattered U.S. and allied ground units for secure communications, imagery, and targeting data;

- Improve the integration and user friendliness of NRO and NSA data and systems used to support operations, targeting, and ISR;[26]

- Modify existing CH-47D Chinook helicopters by adding refueling probes, additional weapons, and radar sensors, allowing them be used by special operations forces.[27]

- Streamline the Navy helicopter fleet from six to two types of helicopters, thereby increasing efficiency and decreasing maintenance costs.[28]

Many of these relevant concepts and capabilities were first proposed during Vietnam, and Afghanistan has probably done more to validate such activities than to initiate them. It also seems realistic to call such progress part of an "evolution in military affairs" instead of a "revolution." The evolution does not, however, make the steady progress and the result any less important or impressive.

MISSION EFFECTIVENESS VERSUS MISSION INTENSITY: THE DUEL BETWEEN OFFENSE AND DEFENSE CONTINUES

Closing the loop in near-real-time intelligence, targeting, precision strike, assessment, and restrike operations may significantly improve mission effectiveness in ways that reduce the need for sheer force numbers and mission intensity. Not only did airpower substitute in many ways for heavy ground forces, armor, and artillery; but precision airpower and far better targeting almost certainly substituted for airpower numbers. Deploying even more effective real-time intelligence, targeting, and damage assessment systems can therefore either make a given force steadily more effective in battle or allow a reduction in force numbers and mission intensity.[29]

Adversaries also make improvements. Important potential countermeasures to advances in U.S. war-fighting capability—advances all too familiar to most military forces in the Middle East—include:

- Smaller and smaller targets and a shift to more distributed forms of warfare;
- Hide or shield operations through increased use of colocation with civilians;
- Constant relocation of operations, making it more difficult to target by function (no advances in technical platforms will be able to compensate for a lack of reliable human intelligence and/or enhanced presence on the ground);
- Dispersal of assets before or during a conflict without any normal indicators of combat operations (as Iraq dispersed chemical weapons near unmanned air facilities during the Gulf War);
- Deployment of distributed mixes of highly advanced surface-to-air missiles—the SA-10 or SA-11, shorter-range systems, sensors, and command-and-control links—to deny effective long-range air strike capabilities; and
- Creation of retaliatory forces with WMD that can be launched on warning or when under attack.

At the same time, there are limits to the adaptations that enemy forces can make in response to improved U.S. capabilities. Large masses of armor, artillery, and combat air assets can scarcely be distributed; indeed, moving them may simply make them targets. Distributed forces are weaker forces, and hiding among civilians is a double-edged sword that may alienate those providing cover. Buying expensive and highly sophisticated air defense systems can also be countered with new targeting and strike technologies. Relying on CBRN weapons as a deterrent is only credible if they cannot be targeted and if it is clear that they will be used.

THE MEDIA AND THE PSYOP BATTLE

The United States was not prepared to conduct a major information campaign at the start of the Afghan War. It had been focused on U.S. and Western media and perceptions; and it lacked area linguists, expertise, and experts who understood both the sensitivities and attitudes of the factions in Afghanistan and the nations around it.

Although senior U.S. officials did make every effort to make it clear the United States was fighting a war against terrorism and not against Islam, the Department of Defense initially used words like "crusade" to describe the campaign and was unprepared for the hostile reaction in parts of the Arab world because of the second Intifada and U.S. ties to Israel.

Senior officials within the Office of the Secretary of Defense admitted on background several months after the start of the war that the United States had done a better job of dealing with the media and psychological dimensions of the war in the terms of the reaction of the U.S. and Western media, but it had been slow to focus on the regional media and deal with psychological operations.

It is not yet clear how the United States can improve its efforts to deal with regional media and strengthen and modernize its psychological operations (PSYOP) capabilities, but this seems to be a significant lesson and one the United States must address with more skill in future wars.

Certain fundamentals must also be addressed. No amount of information management can substitute for better methods of minimizing civilian casualties and collateral damage. The same is true of peacekeeping and nation building. No amount of media can be a substitute for the presence of trained experts on the ground that can both work with local groups and factions and help U.S. commanders understand local sensitivities and problems. Understanding and dealing with the local aspects of asymmetric warfare is critical to victory.

At the same time, information warfare has a global, regional, and theaterwide dimension, and the United States is still trying to find the proper tools to deal with this issue. The White House did create an interagency Coalition Information Center, or war room, to try to handle the media and information dimension of the war. This office helped coordinate the U.S. effort to shape the information aspects of the war and address Islamic and cultural sensitivities. It helped with speech writing, the symbols used in U.S. documents, U.S. recognition of Islamic holidays, and visits with Islamic officials. Although such a center cannot hope to convert the critics and enemies of the United States and the details of its operation are still unclear, it does seem to be a model for future conflicts.[30] Creating such an office the moment a major conflict seems likely, staffing it with sufficiently senior personnel to reach policymakers, and providing both interagency representatives and regional experts may be a way of ensuring the U.S. government engages the world and not simply its domestic audience and sympathetic allies.

The Department of Defense provided a wide range of daily civilian and military briefings and ensured that senior U.S. officials and commanders kept in touch with the media. This had a powerful impact on domestic and Western perceptions of the fighting. In general, however, the Defense Department had far less success in sending its message to the region. Its handling of issues like friendly and civilian casualties and collateral damage remained awkward—in part because it simply did not have accurate data on a timely basis. The Defense Department lacked the expertise to work well with regional media and to support foreign broadcasts and media in local languages. The Voice of America, in contrast, often seemed to lack suitable military expertise and information.

The Defense Department's failed attempt to create the Office of Strategic Influence was its effort to create a new structure to manage this part of the conflict. Its very title, however, as well as the way in which it was proposed created the image of an office of propaganda and fears that it would be used to issue lies and carry out deception campaigns. Reaction against the idea was so great that it had to be abandoned.[31] It is far from clear how this office would have interacted with the U.S. State Department and the Voice of America or how it would have carried out systematic information or propaganda efforts to deal with the U.S. and foreign media and public opinion.[32] The basic concept seems sound in many ways, but the execution will need to be far more careful and better planned.

Theater efforts to deal with these issues were more successful. Having Green Berets, Special Forces, and other U.S. military personal on the ground to improve relations and win over the "minds and hearts" of the Afghan people proved to be critical. The United States used both PSYOP teams and specially trained military personnel in the Afghan countryside to search for possible political problems, interact with local military leaders and village elders, and assist Afghan civilians in distress. By interacting with the civilian population, these PSYOP teams helped create local support and reduced support for Al Qaeda and the Taliban. Military and diplomatic efforts to reach out to the media and deal with local problems and sensitivities proved to be equally critical. In a number of cases, however, the United States was badly short of personnel with the proper skills and area expertise and was slow to recognize that the political dimension of the battle was as critical as the tactical dimension.

The U.S. military services also have a long tradition of talking about area expertise and information warfare and then going on to underfund and undersize such efforts, leaving them out of contingency plans and making them poor career paths. Like improvements in the funding and quality of intelligence analysts and HUMINT, talk is cheap and action is often lacking. Most of the discussion of net-centric warfare, for example, ignores the critical importance of the military having area experts, PSYOP experts, and trained teams to work with coalition partners. Talk of net-centric warfare usually focuses on the physical dimension of targeting and not on the personal, psychological, and local political realities of net-centric, asymmetric, and coalition warfare. Even military literature often focuses on the "snake-eating" aspects of Special Forces and field teams like the Green Berets that work in the field with coalition allies. The fact that many snake eaters have masters' degrees and can act as linguists and intelligence officers is often ignored.

The fact remains, however, that Afghanistan is only one recent conflict that shows that no RMA can be solely technology based. Advances in technology in areas like ISR and precision weapons must be coupled not only to the integration of HUMINT and better intelligence analysis skills but also to political and psychological warfare, military advisory efforts, peacekeeping efforts, and civil-military operations at every level—and especially at the theater and tactical levels in the field. The possibilities of new conflicts involving Iraq, the Taiwan Strait, and Korea and peacekeeping involving situations like the second Intifada make the point. Without addressing such issues, it is also pointless to talk about tactical interoperability with allies in asymmetric warfare and to consider coalition warfare with allies from other cultures.

There will always be limits on what can be done. No amount of PSYOP and information warfare can persuade enemies, create only friends, and disarm critics. At the same time, the U.S. government as a whole and the Department of Defense in particular need to assign a higher priority to these areas of activity, organize more formal and lasting structures to deal with these aspects of conflict, and create pools of the necessary mix of expertise that can be assembled rapidly and put into action the moment a conflict seems likely. Force transformation cannot be fully successful without such an effort, and asymmetric war will always present special challenges in winning the information battle.

War does involve deception, half-truths, and sometimes lies. In blunt terms, it is better to lie than kill. The problem is to strike the proper balance and use such aspects of information warfare and tactics only when they are necessary. Finding this balance will never be easy and failures will always occur. However, creating real expertise and a clear structure for handling such issues is one way to ensure that the United States makes the best possible effort to use information warfare, deception, and PSYOP effectively and wisely.

USMC, THE OSPREY, THE AV-8B, AND NONLITTORAL WARFARE

The U.S. Marine Corps faces a potential crisis over the reliability and cost of the Osprey; the readiness and effectiveness of the AV-8B; and the need to modernize many aspects of its transport helicopter, combat aviation, land systems, and amphibious systems. In spite of the increase in defense spending under the FY 2003–2007 defense program, it is not clear that the Marine Corps will get the funding it needs to be able to sustain air operations properly in a major regional contingency like Iraq. Some long overdue force improvements—like adding the LITENING 2 infrared targeting pods to the AV-8B—will help in some ways, but such improvements will not necessarily correct problems of range, sustainability, and reliability.[33]

At the same time, the USMC role in Afghanistan raises issues about the need to plan for more nonlittoral operations and to create real Special Forces capabilities with language, area, and advisory expertise. The success of the U.S. Army Special Forces and Ranger units and the Marine Corps forces in Afghanistan may well show that the so-called lessons of Task Force Hawk in the Kosovo conflict and the resulting failure to commit U.S. Army light and attack helicopter forces in Kosovo may not be lessons at all, but rather the result of political decisions and unique training and readiness problems. Certainly, the U.S. Army's ability to airlift and drop more than 200 rangers and intelligence officers into Taliban-controlled territory in Operation Rhino on October 19, 2001, indicates that properly planned assault operations can be very effective. More important, the AH-64 emerged as a critical weapon and provided critical close air support in the fighting at Shah-i-Kot.[34]

There seems to be a good case for examining how force transformation and a shift to longer-range strike and airmobile operations should affect the future of the Marine Corps. In particular, it is not clear that present programs call for a proper level of modernization in attack-helicopter and airmobile forces and for improving their capability to conduct counterterrorism and asymmetric warfare missions—missions that seem likely to be a key aspect of future combat in the Middle East.

USE OF CARRIERS AND SURFACE SHIPS AS BASES FOR SPECIAL FORCES AND LAND OPERATIONS

As successful as USN carrier operations were during the fighting in Afghanistan, they were heavily dependent on USAF air assets based in Bahrain, Qatar, the UAE, and Oman. Even during the Gulf War, questions arose about the need for longer-range carrier strike attack aircraft that could carry more weapons, deliver them with maximum accuracy, avoid having to return with munitions loads or dump munitions, and reduce the burden on USAF refueling assets.

The campaign in Afghanistan saw the use of the carrier *Kitty Hawk* as an afloat forward-staging base (AFSB) for Special Forces assets that included more than 1,000 personnel from the Navy SEALs, Army and Air Force special operations units, Army Green Berets, and the 160th Special Operations Aviation Regiment as well as the rotary aircraft—the MH-60 Blackhawk, MH-47 Chinook, and MH-53 Pave Low—that accompany these forces.[35] This allowed better command and control of Special Forces operations, provided joint basing and command facilities, and allowed for better management of helicopter assets. At the same time, however, use of the *Kitty Hawk* in this way reduced by one the number of carriers available for standard operations, decreased overall Navy strike capability, affected training schedules, and forced other carriers to compensate for its absence by extending their own deployments.[36]

The ability to transform a carrier into a mobile piece of sovereign U.S. territory is useful, but the Navy is exploring options that will allow this to occur without affecting overall carrier strike capabilities and readiness. One option being considered is delaying the decommissioning of the USS *Constellation* and refitting it for specific use by Special Forces. Another option involves taking a large, medium-speed roll-on–roll-off (LMSR) ship and converting it to handle helicopters in addition to its current transport and cargo capabilities. A final option is to lease a commercial vessel and modify its hull to meet the necessary specifications for use as an AFSB.

Far too little attention seems to be given to using the larger amphibious ships of the Marine Corps for this kind of mission; possibly this is caused by relatively parochial service reasons. In many contingencies, however, the United States will need its entire pool of active carriers without needing its entire pool of amphibious operations. A true joint approach to this issue would examine the amphibious option. Moreover, using Marine Corps amphibious vessels at such times might help push the corps toward creating true Special Forces units and integrating their operations with the other services.

Regardless of which option is chosen, the use of carriers as AFSBs represents an evolution in the role of the carrier in military operations and represents the military's desire to increase U.S. power projection and strike capability across the globe, thereby complementing attempts to create a new forward-deployed military deterrence against future enemies.[37]

The experiment in use of AFSBs is part of ongoing efforts by the Navy's Deep Blue operations group, which is charged with examining and developing new weapons platforms and systems, sensors, and tactics to increase U.S. capabilities against Al Qaeda and other unconventional opponents. Deep Blue is specifically analyzing how to further integrate special operations forces into future Navy combat missions and operations. Deep Blue is also evaluating options for increasing the deployment time—from 12 months to 18 months—of destroyer and cruiser squadrons.[38]

As part of its efforts to increase the role of Special Forces in Navy operations, the Navy has been working on developing and deploying minisubs that are designed to carry up to eight SEALs with scuba and combat gear. Currently, SEALs are deployed in open vessels where they are exposed to both the elements and possibly enemy fire. The minisub, providing SEALs with a more secure transport environment, would solve this problem. The development and deployment progress for the project, however, is far behind schedule and far over cost. Although the minisub is light enough to be transported on a C-17 or C-5 aircraft, its development history exemplifies of the hurdles that must be overcome as part of transforming the military.[39]

Afghanistan also presents a basic question of the cost-effectiveness of using nuclear submarines as platforms for small special operations teams. The argument for giving such expensive ships more mission capabilities if they are needed for other purposes may be a good one; but the proposal that such small mission elements, with such limited ability to cover the world, justify maintaining and tailoring nuclear submarines for this role seems to be more a desperate effort by the Navy's submariners to maintain the size and prestige of their part of the Navy than anything approaching a cost-effective use of funds.

TRUE JOINTNESS FOR THE NAVY AND MARINE CORPS

The fact that carriers were once again so important to fighter attack missions illustrates the need for the Navy and Marine Corps to move forward as quickly as possible to implement several of the nine capability goals the U.S. Navy identified in its *Seapower 21* study and the March 2002 draft of its force transformation plan, "Power and Access from the Sea."[40] These include goals—such as persistent ISR, time-critical strike, compressed deployment and employment time, and offensive information operations—with obvious relevance to Afghanistan. At the same time, any reader of such Navy material must conclude that it is still relatively parochial and seapower oriented, not joint-operations oriented.

The USA and USAF are scarcely free of service parochialism, but the Navy's literature does not truly address flexibility and depth of operations and the need to support the other services in joint warfare. This is particularly dangerous at a time when fleet size continues to shrink at a rate that could produce a battle fleet of fewer than 260 ships.[41] There are good reasons to question the sheer scale and rate of such downsizing, but the Navy's natural desire to preserve its most advanced ships and its technological edge seems to have led it to turn its force transformation exercise into a study of how it can best advance seapower, not how it can best deal with joint warfare in cases like Afghanistan, Iraq, Korea, or a major attack across the Taiwan Strait.

CARRIER OPERATIONS AND AIRCRAFT PERFORMANCE

Concurrently and more generally, the U.S. Navy and U.S. Marine Corps need to examine closely the real-world performance of the JSF in light of the history of operations in Afghanistan, mission requirements in the Middle East, and possible reductions in the U.S. ability to base USAF tankers and other support aircraft forward in their present numbers. This relook at the capability of the JSF does not seem likely to mean radical changes in the role of the carrier per se, but it does mean rethinking these aspects of USN and USMC combat air operations and particularly the capabilities and associated systems of the JSF to see how these aspects of sea-based strike capabilities can be improved over time.

Closing the loop in terms of the ability to improve targeting and the ability of the Navy and the Marine Corps to use airpower to deliver precision guided munitions effectively and with maximum strategic and tactical impact is of more value in carrier operations than other air operations. There are finite limits—in terms of both peak and sustained operations—to carrier sortie rates. The fact that three carriers sustained an average of fewer than 70 attack sorties per day during the peak of the Afghan fighting is in some ways an illustration of this point.

So is the fact that the Navy flew 4,900 of the 6,500 strike sorties between October 7 and December 17, 2001, or 75 percent of the total—and struck at an estimated 2,000 mobile targets but delivered less than 30 percent of the ordnance. As of June 2002 this ratio remained largely the same, with the Navy estimating that although it had flown 75 percent of the total sorties during the Afghan conflict, the USAF had dropped 75 percent of the total ordnance from heavy bombers.[42]

The fact also remains that "antique" B-52s and B-1s flew 10 percent of the missions from Diego Garcia but delivered 11,500 of the 17,500 weapons dropped—65 percent of all weapons dropped and 89 percent of all weapons dropped by the USAF. While the bombers dropped the vast majority of the 6,500 500-pound dumb bombs used, they also dropped roughly half of all the guided munitions.[43] It is far from clear that bombers could operate as easily in a less permissive air defense environment, but the same is equally true of carrier strike aircraft.

Making individual sorties more effective is not only the most cost-effective way of dealing with these limitations; it also is the best way of dealing with the complications of a steadily increasing need to reduce civilian casualties, reduce collateral damage, and deal with steadily more complex asymmetric wars.

CHEAP CRUISE MISSILES AND NAVAL STRIKE POWER

Although no precise unclassified data are yet available, it seems clear that GPS-guided cruise missiles in Afghanistan were far more reliable and accurate than the terrain contour matching (TERCOM) radar mapping versions that were used in the Gulf War. GPS-guided cruise missiles were also much easier and more flexible to target, and had much less predictable flight paths.

The Afghan War again raises questions about the sheer cost of the cruise missile and the best way to arm the kind of arsenal ship represented by the DD(X). It is an irony of the cruise missile that the U.S. Navy needs more and more long-range strike assets but only a relatively few targets merit strike systems that cost nearly $1 million per round. The Navy seems to have a very high regional priority for cost engineering some form of cruise missile that comes closer to the cost level of $200,000.

FINDING ADEQUATE ELECTRONIC WARFARE ASSETS

The continuing delays in replacing the EA-6B and what may be serious engine-life problems also illustrate the need to rethink carrier strike operations in terms of the ability to deliver Afghan War–like persistence over target with suitable electronic warfare protection.

The problems with a limited force of EA-6Bs also raise general questions about the combined capability of the USN, USAF, and USMC to deploy enough electronic warfare assets. This already was a problem in Kosovo, and it is far from clear that current programs will succeed to the point where they ensure future survivability in an air environment in which nations like Iraq have dense surface-to-air missile assets in some areas and other nations like Iran may acquire systems like the SA-400. The permissive environment that allowed aircraft like the AC-130 to enjoy near freedom of operations over Afghanistan may not exist in future contingencies in the Middle East.

THE MARINE CORPS, THE LHA-X, LHD-X, THE ARMY, AND MARITIME PRE-POSITIONING

Amphibious capability and maritime pre-positioning may become even more important in the future in the Middle East if the United States cannot establish the kind of support for coalition operations it needs from Egypt and the Gulf states. The United States also faces a potential legal problem in terms of the British ability to maintain sovereignty over Diego Garcia. At the same time, the Army is lightening its power projection forces, raising questions about the future force mix, the role of Marine Corps forces, and the extent to which amphibious ships and pre-positioning ships should support a given mix of Marine Corps and Army forces.

These are not issues that affect the Middle East alone. Any regional force planning exercise should examine force transformation options for changing the overall mix of Marine Corps and Army land forces; the possibility of standardization on some equipment like LAVs and light artillery; and new mixes of amphibious and maritime pre-positioning capability that could be more effective than the present mix of capabilities in the Mediterranean Sea, Indian Ocean, and Persian Gulf.

The increasingly awkward and artificial split between an expeditionary Marine Corps and a U.S. Army seeking to transform itself to perform an identical mission also raises serious questions. The Marine Corps has historical reason to fear that transforming itself to perform sustained missions in addition to amphibious and littoral warfare can lead to green-eyeshade challenges to its independence and force size. There does seem to be an endless supply of accountants who ignore on narrow cost-effectiveness grounds the unique and proven combat capabilities of the Marine Corps. Nevertheless, if the Army needs to go light and fast, Afghanistan indicates the Marine Corps may need to go deeper, go land, and have more firepower and sustainment.

At the same time, the amphibious fleet and ships in the present amphibious readiness groups could be used more flexibly. The use of the *Kitty Hawk* to provide a base for Army Special Forces is only one way of providing such a capability. The Key West agreement defining the present roles and missions of the services has no functional meaning. If Army forces can make better use of Navy platforms than can the Marine Corps in any given contingency, it is the Army forces that should use the Navy platforms. Conversely, the United States should not pay to convert U.S. Army units to light forces if the mission can be performed by a restructured set of Marine Corps forces with the capability of sustaining operations for longer periods with heavier equipment. These factors need to be considered in designing both future amphibious ships and pre-positioning ships like the Military Sealift Command's Army LMSR logistic ship.

This raises the question of seeking a pattern of force transformation in which maritime and land pre-positioning can provide a more standardized equipment mix that can be used by both the Marine Corps and the Army. A capabilities-based force, emphasizing rapid expeditionary operations and lighter weapons, would be far more flexible if the U.S. Army and U.S. Marine Corps systematically became more interoperable. The ability to deal with multiple simultaneous contingencies, including unexpected areas, would be much greater.

The U.S. force transformation exercises seem to have avoided asking any fundamental questions about the overall Army–Marine Corps force mix. Afghanistan indicates that these questions need to be asked.

U.S. ARMY AND FUTURE COMBAT SYSTEMS

Afghanistan raises broad questions about the U.S. Army force mix. While the Afghan War is being used to justify the U.S. Army's effort to transform its present armored and mechanized power projection forces into forces with much lighter armor and artillery that can be moved and deployed much more rapidly, it is far from clear that the Afghan conflict provides a good reason for this action or that even an increased level of defense spending will allow the U.S. Army to accomplish such a force transformation on a timely basis.[44]

The FY 2003 budget request encourages some important programs and cancels others. It calls for procurement of 332 interim armored vehicles (at a cost of $935.9 million) and the creation of a new six-brigade force based on 20-ton wheeled vehicles. This plan calls for one brigade capable of deploying anywhere in the world by C-130 within four days, and a four-brigade division within 30 days.[45] Serious questions also exist regarding the weight of these "light" systems and the fact that they are so large that they impose virtually the same capacity limits on existing lift as do current "heavy" systems.

The Army will also spend $717 million on the development of a future combat system to create a far more advanced rapidly deployable set of Army ground forces—evidently to be deployed at some point well beyond 2010. Other improvements are planned for items like unmanned ground combat vehicles and medium tactical vehicles, although the experience in Afghanistan indicates that much of the planned fleet may still be too heavy and too large and may lack the needed all-terrain mobility for a similar contingency.[46]

To help fund these changes, the Army is canceling some 18 programs during FY 2003–2006 because it says they do not fit into the future objective force.[47] Some are heavy systems like the Crusader that do not affect the Army's ability to meet the need demonstrated in Afghanistan for more effective light forces. About half the canceled programs, however, are light systems or programs like the battlefield combat identification system that do seem to mesh with the lessons of the conflict.

At the same time, the Army will still spend a great deal on older, heavy, legacy systems.[48] It also does not seem to have clear plans for Army aviation: No new attack helicopter is in sight and the endless "development" of the Comanche continues, but improvements will be made to the AH-64A/D attack helicopters The integration of UAVs and UCAVs has been encouraged by the Army's experience in Afghanistan, but the Army is far from having a meaningful force plan to make use of such systems.

The key question is whether the Army can actually resolve its internal debate and its debate with the Office of the Secretary of Defense and manage a smooth transition to more mobile forces and lighter equipment.[49] It could well end up with a future combat system that may look desirable but still takes far too long to actually deploy and remains dependent on an awkward mix of legacy and interim systems—many of which would be too heavy and others of which would be light but too large to produce any saving in air or sealift because they would be cubic limited instead of weight limited. For example, as of March 2002, eight of the ten new light Stryker armored vehicles were still too heavy for airlift in a C-130.[50]

SPECIAL FORCES, LIGHT FORCES, AND AIR ASSAULT FORCES

The performance of attack helicopters and U.S. Army Special Forces and Ranger units illustrates that the so-called lessons of Task Force Hawk and the failure to commit U.S. Army light and attack helicopter forces in Kosovo are not really lessons at all. They instead seem to be the result of political decisions and unique training and readiness problems.

In Afghanistan, the 101st Airborne and other light and highly mobile U.S. and allied ground troops had consistent success wherever they were engaged, even under near-worst-case conditions like the opening engagements in Operation Anaconda. Attack helicopters proved to be rapidly deployable, survivable, and highly effective.

The role of the AC-130 has had so much public exposure that it scarcely needs further analysis. Special Forces have been of critical importance, however, in a number of other areas. Two small Special Forces A teams played a critical role in allowing the United States to work with friendly Afghans and in illuminating targets with an effectiveness that no amount of ISR technology could possibly have equaled.[51] Larger elements of U.S. and allied Special Forces have played a continuing role in operating against Al Qaeda and the Taliban in areas where local Afghans are potentially hostile and other forces could not be brought into play without massive additional manpower and support. U.S. and allied Special Forces also served well in the border area of Pakistan and several Central Asian states.[52]

Special Forces provided a critical element of coalition warfare in training Afghan forces and in providing local intelligence. They also played an equally critical role in keeping Afghan factions apart and in dealing with local rivalries and tensions. Nothing could have avoided serious problems in this regard, but the result might have been disastrous if Special Forces had not mediated and kept apart various Afghan factions.

The U.S. Army's demonstration on October 19, 2001, of its ability to airlift and drop more than 200 Rangers and intelligence officers into Taliban-controlled territory in Operation Rhino may have been largely a pointless exercise in showboating, but it may also have indicated that properly planned airborne operations might be effective. A good case can be made for examining the expansion of Special and Ranger Forces, modernizing their equipment, and tailoring attack helicopter and airmobile forces for counterterrorism and asymmetric warfare missions.

The fact that the combined impact of Afghanistan and a small operation in the Philippines seriously depleted the total inventory of MH-60Ks and MH-47Es owing to minimal combat losses and accidents certainly indicates that the United States had badly undercapitalized its Special Forces before the war began.[53] Delays in upgrading the MH-47s and the MH-53 Pave Low helicopter may well have contributed to these problems although they were partly the result of the long delays in delivering the CV-22. Troops also experienced lesser equipment problems—the two Special Forces teams that played a critical role in targeting early in the conflict initially had laser illuminators but not the equipment needed to provide accurate GPS coordinates for targeting purposes.[54]

While press account are uncertain, the U.S. Special Operations Command (SOCOM) has asked for major new resources as the result of events in Afghanistan and the war on terrorism. SOCOM sought a budget of $4.89 billion in FY 2003—some $890 million more than in FY 2002—and projected a rise to nearly $6 billion in FY 2003. It nearly doubled its procurement request from $400.5 million to $776.8 million and raised its research, development, test, and evaluation (RDT&E) request from $392 million to $431 million. Largely as a result of Afghanistan, the U.S. Army began examining requirements for:[55]

- Lightweight countermortar radars that two soldiers can carry in parts and assemble in 30 minutes;

- Collapsible UAVs that are portable by personnel or small vehicles and are suitable for both rural and urban warfare;

- Better, smaller, lighter, longer-range, and air-droppable laser designators;

- Improved communications for direct field communications in cities and in rough, mountainous terrain;

- Better and dedicated designs for light ATVs; in the past, because the HMMWV proved to be too large for local roads and terrain and made the user a highly visible target, Special Forces had to buy Toyota trucks and use recreational four-wheeled ATVs made by the Polaris Corporation; and

- Lighter, smaller, and more enduring batteries.

There are, of course, many other tactical, technical, and equipment lessons, and it is too early to do more than note that the United States cannot afford to learn such lessons and then act upon them.

The war in Afghanistan also highlighted several issue needing urgent examination regarding the future role of Special Forces. Although some of the issues do not need public discussion, an equal case can be made for reexamining the role that CIA operations should play as well as the interface between the CIA and Special Forces.

It might also an appropriate time to reexamine how Special Forces are commanded and integrated into policy. At present, gaps seem to exist among the service commands; military command of SOF; civilians in special operations, low-intensity conflict (SOLIC); and the policy offices under the secretary of defense. In practice, it is clear that Special Forces are primarily a tool for joint warfare, but the issue of exactly who is in charge at the top is one that needs to be resolved by putting someone clearly in charge. The last thing on earth the Special Forces need is either an overcomplicated chain of command or one that is overpoliticized.

The role of the Marine Corps in Special Forces is also an issue. Before the fighting in Afghanistan, the Marine Corps had decided to create a specialized combat unit—similar to the Army's Rangers and Green Berets—that was to be committed to SOCOM. The first 42 Marines were sent to SOCOM in January 2002.[56]

Although the post-Afghan Special Forces objectives of the Marine Corps have not been established, a main area of focus will be enhancing USMC high-speed special operations and reconnaissance abilities. Given the level of joint operations with Army and Navy Special

Forces that the Marine Corps has been involved in during the fighting in Afghanistan, the creation of a Marine Corps special operations unit that can more closely interact with other special forces is a natural next step. Such a unit will allow for better execution of future joint missions as it decreases the communications and information problems that can sometimes occur in an operation involving forces from multiple services.[57]

GLOBAL, REGIONAL, AND THEATER COMMAND

The Pentagon is already examining ways to create some form of global command, which is needed to coordinate the new battle against terrorism and asymmetric warfare. It is also seeking better ways to solve the complex problem of tying together intelligence, the management of coalition warfare, and conducting the political-military aspects of asymmetric wars as well as the need for finding better ways to coordinate new forms of air-ground operations. Secretary Rumsfeld has such an effort under way.

Afghanistan shows, however, that creating an effective regional and in-theater command structure is equally important and is a critical factor in making optimal use of ISR and precision-weapons assets. In retrospect, modern communications and ISR assets did not allow for effective command from remote locations, and factors as simple as the differences in time zones and a lack of satellite bandwidth became problems.

In Desert Storm approximately 2,000 personnel were required to handle air operations, but during the conflict in Afghanistan roughly 1,500 personnel have coordinated operations. The Air Force chief of staff, Gen. John Jumper, would like to see that number decrease as advanced technology systems, offering significantly improved ISR capabilities, replace human operators. The eventual goal is to make AOCs smaller and more portable and possibly integrate them with naval assets. This will allow for greater flexibility in conducting air operations in remote locations and decrease U.S. dependence on other nations that must agree to host and allow the United States to conduct operations from AOCs located within their borders.[58]

Creating large, fixed facilities like the CAOC in Saudi Arabia has led to political and access problems and has meant using facilities tailored for other purposes. This argues for a more forward and expeditionary approach to regional and theater command. This also argues for sea-based joint—not Navy-Marine Corps—command capabilities.

At the same time, much of the U.S. combat experience in Afghanistan argues for establishing joint—not service—commands at every level and for using ISR and C^{4}I/BM assets to improve support to the theater and tactical commanders rather than as a means to try to manage the war from Washington or a distant regional command. Technology creates natural and destructive tendencies to try to micromanage from the rear, add or centralize layers of decision making, and increase the time for decision making. Effective net-centric and near-real-time warfare, however, requires virtually the opposite use of technology. Line-of-sight command may be obsolete, but forward and on-the-scene command is not. The National Command Authority that manages least, manages best; and it produces a major saving in the communications burden and sheer bandwidth.

COUNTERPROLIFERATION AND PREEMPTION

The problem of CBRN warfare has already been addressed in terms of targeting and weapons requirements. The discovery of a large-scale Al Qaeda effort to develop CBRN weapons—as well as ongoing proliferation in nations like Iran, Iraq, and North Korea—illustrates the steadily growing importance of offensive counterproliferation capabilities as well as preemption or immediate, time-urgent attack the moment combat begins.

Preemption and large-scale initial destruction are not actions that can be advocated carelessly or that should lead to the use of weapons without concern for political sensitivities, civilian casualties, and collateral damage. Proliferation and CBRN threats do, however, fundamentally change the risks and values of war. Proliferators give their enemies the right to preemption and first strikes simply by proliferating; and the axiom that the only way to go to war with the United States is with the possession of nuclear weapons is an axiom the

United States must aggressively counter, regardless of whether a nation or terrorist movement is involved.

Waiting for enemy assets to be dispersed can also create an impossible tactical burden. Note that the United States flew some 2,400 sorties searching for and trying to strike at dispersed Iraqi Scud missiles during the Gulf War. On approximately 42 occasions, U.S. aircraft spotted a launch plume, and aircraft made eight actual attacks. Nevertheless, neither coalition airpower nor Special Forces damaged a single Scud. Iraq was able to fire some 88 Scuds against Israel and Saudi Arabia.[59]

The threat of biological warfare is particularly serious, and the United States and its allies need to rethink internal security planning, public health response, and defense efforts to deal with the broad range of CBRN threats. The examples of hoof-and-mouth disease and mad-cow disease are almost models of how not to deal with such cooperation and are a warning of how much more effort is needed to deal with both time-urgent tactical threats and the broad spectrum of global threats.

That said, it is one thing to have a doctrine and plans and quite another to have a capability. Any form of attack on CBRN and their delivery system assets must involve meaningful targeting capability, the proper weapons and destructive means, and careful consideration of civilian casualties and collateral damage. The United States could not carry out a successful attack on Iraq's CBRN assets at either the time of the Gulf War or Desert Fox. It had no idea of what to target at the beginning of the Afghan conflict.

Moreover, the very prospect of such attacks pushes other countries to create launch-on-warning (LOW) and launch-under-attack (LUA) capabilities in a use-or-lose environment as well as organize and pre-position assets for terrorist and unconventional attacks.

RETHINKING ARMS AND EXPORT CONTROLS

Much of the debate over chemical warfare, the Anti-Ballistic Missile Treaty, the Biological Weapons Convention, and the Comprehensive Test Ban Treaty has focused on large-scale conventional war fighting.

The debate has avoided coming to grips, in detail, with the threat of asymmetric attacks and terrorism.

The same has been true of export controls. A joint effort at comprehensive review of how to change arms control agreements and export controls—looking at the CBRN and advanced technology threat as a whole—is needed to develop a more effective common strategy.

It is at the same time a dangerous illusion to assume that any revision in either export controls or arms control agreements can deal with the problem of chemical, biological, and possibly nuclear proliferation. The literature on this subject is more well meaning than technically competent, and little effort seems to have been made to carry out realistic net technical assessments of how rapidly the dissemination of skills and equipment related to biotechnology, pharmaceuticals, and food processing—coupled to advances in areas like genetic engineering—will allow most governments in the developing world and many terrorists to create biological weapons that provide little or no warning and possess nuclear levels of lethality.

The same is true of somewhat similar trends affecting the ability to make third- and fourth-generation chemical weapons and assemble a nuclear device if fissile material can be obtained from the outside. Similarly, covert delivery means are far easier to create than are ballistic missiles, and they may often be a far more desirable method of delivery.

The efforts of Al Qaeda may have been as badly organized as those of Aum Shinrikyo, but they are a warning and not a guarantee for the future. Indigenous proliferation, possibly under breakout conditions with limited or no warning, is becoming a global reality.

NOTES

[1] *Defense News*, January 14–20, pp. 3, 28; *Inside the Pentagon*, January 31, 2001, p. 1.

[2] See Kim Burger and Andrew Koch, "Afghanistan: the Key Lessons," *Jane's Defense Weekly*, January 2, 2001, pp. 20–27.

[3] *Financial Times*, January 21, 2002, p. 15.

[4] *Jane's Defense Weekly*, January 2, 2001, p. 23.

⁵ *Jane's Defense Weekly,* January 2, 2001, pp. 22–23.

⁶ *Los Angeles Times,* July 13, 2002.

⁷ Ibid.; July 14, 2002, p. M-1.

⁸ *Los Angeles Times,* July 13, 2002.

⁹ Ibid.; *Defense News,* July 15, 2002, p.10.

¹⁰ *Los Angeles Times,* July 14, 2002, p. M-1.

¹¹ *Los Angeles Times,* July 13, 2002; *Defense News,* July 15, 2002, p.10.

¹² *Defense News,* February 11–17, 2002, pp. 3

¹³ Defense News.com, July 9, 2002.

¹⁴ *Navy Times,* July 22, 2002, p. 8.

¹⁵ *Baltimore Sun,* July 10, 2002.

¹⁶ For a broader summary of U.S force transformation activity, see Hans Binnendijk and Richard Kugler, "Adapting Forces to a New Era: Ten Transforming Concepts," *Defense Horizons,* no. 5, Center for Technology and National Security Policy, National Defense University, November 2001.

¹⁷ Mait and Grossman, "Relevancy and Risk," p. 4.

¹⁸ *London Times,* January 23, 2002; *Los Angeles Times,* February 10, 2002.

¹⁹ *Jane's Defense Weekly,* January 2, 2001, pp. 20–27.

²⁰ Ibid.

²¹ Bloomberg.com, January 22, 2002; *Los Angeles Times,* January 21, 2002, p. 1.

²² *Los Angeles Times,* January 21, 2002, p. 1.

²³ *Jane's Defense Weekly,* January 2, 2001, pp. 20–27.

²⁴ *Defense News,* February 11–17, 2002, p. 28.

²⁵ *Aviation Week & Space Technology,* January 21, 2002, p. 27.

²⁶ Ibid.

²⁷ *Defense News,* April 8–14, 2002, p. 4.

²⁸ *Norfolk-Virginian Pilot,* July 11, 2002.

²⁹ For broader update on ISR and digital warfare, see Vernon Loeb and Thomas E. Ricks, "1s and 0s Replacing Bullets in the U.S. Arsenal," *Washington Post,* February 2, 2002, p. A-1.

³⁰ *USA Today,* December 19, 2001, p. 14; *Baltimore Sun,* January 23, 2002; Washington Times, January 23, 2002, p. 8.

³¹ *Washington Times,* February 21, 2002, p. 4; *Inside the Pentagon,* February 21, 2002.

[32] *Inside the Pentagon,* February 12, 2002, p. 1; *Washington Times,* February 21, 2002, p. 4; *Washington Post,* February 21, 2002, p. 15; *New York Times,* February 21, 2002, p. 1.

[33] *Defense News,* February 18–24, 2002, p. 26.

[34] *Army Times,* March 25, 2002, p. 15; *Inside the Army,* March 18, 2002, p. 1.

[35] *Washington Post,* December 24, 2002, p. A-8; *New York Times,* April 6, 2002.

[36] *Defense Daily International,* January 18, 2002; *Defense Daily,* July 9, 2002.

[37] Ibid.

[38] *Defense Daily,* February 14, 2002.

[39] Bloomberg News, July 11, 2002.

[40] For a good summary, see *Defense News,* April 15, 2002, p. 8; and *Jane's Defense Weekly,* June 19, 2002, p. 3.

[41] For a broader discussion of these long-standing problems, see Scott C. Truver, "US Navy Programme Review," *Jane's Defense Weekly,* April 4, 2001, pp. 23–28. Also see *Defense News,* June 3, 2002, p. 6.

[42] *Defense Daily,* July 9, 2002, p. 3.

[43] *Los Angeles Times,* February 10, 2002; Gen. Tommy Franks's testimony to the Senate Armed Services Committee on February 7, 2002.

[44] It is impossible to do more than touch upon these issues in this paper. For more details, see the various reports on the U.S. Army's force transformation activities on the Association of the U.S. Army Web page, www.ausa.org, and the official U.S. Army reporting in the Army Web page at www.army.mil.

[45] Great Britain is also developing lighter platforms like the future command and liaison vehicle and the future rapid effects system. *Defense News,* June 17, 2002, p. 18.

[46] See *Defense News,* March 4, 2002, pp. 7, 13; May 20, 2002, p. 26; and *Jane's International Defense Review,* April 2, 2002, p. 21.

[47] *Defense News,* February 18–24, 2002, p. 6.

[48] *Defense News,* February 11–17, 2002, p. 28.

[49] For an interesting summary of the internal and external debate, see Peter J. Boyer, "A Different War," *The New Yorker,* July 1, 2002, pp. 54–67.

[50] *Defense News,* March 2002, p. 7.

[51] *Washington Post,* February 20, 2002, p. A-1; May 19, 2002, p. A-16.

[52] *European Stars and Stripes,* June 19, 2002; *USA Today,* April 29, 2002, p. 8; *Newsweek,* May 13, 2002; *Washington Post,* December 11, 2001, p. A-1; May 5, 2002, p. A-1; *Los Angeles Times,* February 24, 2002, p. 1; March 27,

2002, p.1; May 5, 2002, p. A-1; *New York Times,* May 6, 2002; *Jane's Defense Weekly,* October 17, 2002, pp. 22–23; *Air Force Times,* April 8, 2002, p. 14; *Boston Globe,* March 31, 2002, p. 1; *New York Times,* March 31, 2002, p. A-13; *Washington Times,* July 12, 2002, p. 1.

[53] *Aviation Week & Space Technology,* March 18, 2002, pp. 28–29.

[54] *Washington Post,* February 20, 2002, p. A-1; *Aviation Week & Space Technology,* March 18, 2002, pp. 28–29.

[55] *Defense News,* February 11, 2002, p. 8.

[56] *Defense News,* June 17–23, 2002, p. 40.

[57] Ibid.

[58] *Inside the Air Force,* July 5, 2002, p. 1.

[59] Barry Watts, "Operations and Effects and Effectiveness," in *Gulf War Air Power Survey,* vol. 2 (Washington, D.C.: GPO, 1993), p. 335; Bowie, "Destroying Mobile Ground Targets in an Anti-Access Environment," p. 3.

CHAPTER SEVEN

OTHER LESSONS AND ISSUES

Lessons, or at least important issues, in additional areas seem to be emerging or to have acquired higher priority because of the U.S. experience in Afghanistan.

ADDITIONAL ARMY LESSONS

In addition to lessons discussed earlier, the following can be drawn from the Army's experiences during the fighting in Afghanistan:[1]

Communications

- Need for smaller, lighter, higher-bandwidth communications systems that are easily transportable;
- Mountainous terrain can interfere with FM, line-of-sight communications; this is a problem that must be resolved or alternative advanced communications systems must be developed;
- Need for more frequent updates of operational picture, so that ISR data can be of maximum benefit; and
- Need to develop interoperability among digital communications systems.

Operational Intelligence

With more access to more information also come additional problems, both in the field and at the command center.

- Understanding of the terrain and the battlefield layout continues to be of importance in anticipating future enemy actions;

- New, more mobile reconnaissance forces must be developed to assist in verifying intelligence from other sources; and
- UAVs can be used not only for intelligence but also to fulfill command-and-control needs.

Fire Support

- Air support for ground operations has not been very effective in certain situations; lightweight, more mobile artillery could respond more rapidly and more effectively; and
- AH-64 Apache helicopters have not been able to hover for lengthy periods of time owing to the high altitude, and they were forced to fire while moving; this required coordination between troops on the ground and the helicopter crew.

Engineer Operations

- More training is needed to increase the speed of runway and equipment repairs; and
- Smaller, more deployable Bobcats, forklifts, compactors, and concrete saws are necessary to decrease construction time.

Mine Operations

- Norwegian flail, U.S. mine clearing/armor protection (MCAP), and mine-sniffing dogs have all been effective in detecting mines; however, U.S. miniflail was not effective;
- Antimine centers must be established more rapidly; and
- Battlefield debris and natural terrain severely reduced the effectiveness of mine detectors.

Force Protection

- The unconventional nature of the conflict, including the divided battlefield, geographic separation, and undefined battle zone, made force protection more difficult; and
- Additional equipment needed for force protection includes wide-angle, handheld, and vehicle-mounted thermal imagers; metal and explosive detectors; prisoner-of-war detainee equipment; and mirrors.

ADDITIONAL NAVY LESSONS

The U.S. Navy also has learned additional lessons from its involvement in Operation Enduring Freedom. These lessons include:[2]

ISR

- Need more connectivity to ISR data for personnel charged with firing weapons;
- Develop ways to transfer P-3 imagery to distant receivers;
- Acquisition and deployment of additional P-3 sensor kits; and
- Acquisition and deployment of additional fleet-based tactical UAVs.

Operations

- Mainstream and standardize maritime intercept operations in training and operations;
- Increase integration between Navy Special Forces assets and Navy conventional forces;
- Standardize combat search-and-rescue operations;
- Standardize and improve close air support procedures and operations; and
- Continue to improve interoperability with other services and coalition partners.

Sustainability Needs

- Increase CENTCOM stockpiles of munitions, especially precision guided type;
- Decrease time needed for reloading Tomahawk cruise missile batteries on ships; and
- Improve system of tracking and distributing spare parts.

NOTES

[1] This is based in part on a summary in *Defense News,* July 9, 2002. For the complete report from which these lessons were drawn, see "Emerging Lessons, Insights, and Observations: Operation Enduring Freedom."

[2] Based in part on a summary in *Defense News,* July 9, 2002.

APPENDIX

LIST OF ACRONYMS

AEW	airborne early warning
AFSB	afloat forward-staging base
AIP	Antisurface Warfare Improvement Program
ALT	air loading team
ANA	Afghan National Army
AOC	air operations center
AOR	area of responsibility
ATV	all-terrain vehicle
AWACS	Airborne Warning and Control System
BM	battle management
BOS	base operations support
C⁴ISR	command, control, communications, computers, and information; and intelligence, surveillance, and reconnaissance
CAOC	Combined Air Operations Center
CAP	combat air patrol
CBRN	chemical, biological, radiological, and nuclear
CEM	combined effects munition
CENTCOM	U.S. Central Command

CEP	circular error probable
CFMCC	coalition forces maritime component commander
CIA	U.S. Central Intelligence Agency
CIMIC	civil-military cooperation
CJCMOTF	Coalition Joint Civil-Military Operations Task Force
CM	consequence management
DARPA	Defense Advanced Research Projects Agency
DPG	defense planning guidance
DSCS	Defense Satellite Communications System
ELINT	electronic intelligence
EMERCOM	emergency response organization (Russia)
FAE	fuel-air explosive
FBI	U.S. Federal Bureau of Investigation
FCS	future combat system
FFTTAA	find-fix-track-target-attack-assess
FLIR	forward-looking infrared sensor
HA	humanitarian assistance
HDBT	hard and deeply buried target
HMMWV	high mobility multipurpose wheeled vehicle
HUMINT	intelligence information acquired from humans
IFF	identification of friend or foe
IR	intermediate-range
ISAF	International Security Assistance Force
ISI	Inter-Services Intelligence (Pakistan)
ISR	intelligence, surveillance, and reconnaissance
JDAM	joint direct attack munition
JSF	joint strike fighter
JSTARS	joint surveillance target attack radar system
JWAC	Joint Warfare Analysis Center

KFOR	Kosovo Peacekeeping Force
LAV	light armored vehicles
LIO	leadership interdiction operation
LMSR	large, medium-speed roll-on–roll-off (ship)
LOCAAS	low-cost autonomous attack system
LOW	launch-on-warning
LUA	launch-under-attack
MC^{2}A	multisensor command-and-control aircraft
MCAP	mine clearing/armor protection
medevac	medical evacuation
Milstar	a joint service satellite communications system
MIO	maritime interception operation
NASA	National Aeronautics and Space Administration
NATO	North Atlantic Treaty Organization
NBC	nuclear, biological, and chemical
NORAD	North American Aerospace Defense Command
NRO	National Reconnaissance Office
NSA	National Security Agency
NSSA	National Security Space Architect
OEF	Operation Enduring Freedom
OFW	Objective Force Warrior
PACOM	Pacific Command
PDM	presidential decision memorandum
PHOTINT	real-time imagery
PJHQ	permanent joint headquarters
POI	program of instruction
PSYOP	psychological operation
QDR	Quadrennial Defense Review
RAMCC	Regional Air Movement Control Center

RDT&E	research, development, test, and evaluation
RMA	revolution in military affairs
ROE	rules of engagement
SAR	search and rescue
SAS	Special Air Service (Great Britain)
SDB	small-diameter bomb
SEAD	suppression of enemy air defense
SEAL	Sea, Air, and Land Force
SFOR	Stabilization Force
SFW	sensor fuzed weapon
SIGINT	signals intelligence
SOCOM	U.S. Special Operations Command
SOF	special operations force
SOLIC	special operations, low-intensity conflict
TDRSS	Tracking and Data Relay Satellite System
TERCOM	terrain contour matching
TLAM	Tomahawk land attack missile
UAE	United Arab Emirates
UAV	unmanned aerial vehicle
UCAV	unmanned combat air vehicle
UGV	unmanned ground vehicle
UN	United Nations
USA	U.S. Army
USAF	United States Air Force
USAID	U.S. Agency for International Development
USMC	U.S. Marine Corps
USN	United States Navy
WCMD	wind-corrected munitions dispenser
WMD	weapons of mass destruction

ABOUT THE AUTHOR

Anthony H. Cordesman holds the Arleigh A. Burke Chair in Strategy at CSIS. He is also a national security analyst for ABC News, and his television commentary has been featured prominently during the Gulf War, Desert Fox, the conflict in Kosovo, and the fighting in Afghanistan. During his time at CSIS, Cordesman has been director of the Gulf Net Assessment Project and the Gulf in Transition study, and principal investigator of the CSIS Homeland Defense Project. He has led studies on national missile defense, asymmetric warfare and weapons of mass destruction, and critical infrastructure protection. He has also written on U.S. defense programs and force transformation, the Western military balance, the nuclear balance, arms control in the Arab-Israeli military balance, the economic stability of North Africa, the Asian military balance, and the proliferation of weapons of mass destruction. He directed the CSIS Middle East Net Assessment Project and acted as codirector of the CSIS Strategic Energy Initiative.

Cordesman is the author of a wide range of studies on U.S. security policy, energy policy, and Middle East policy, a number of which are available on the CSIS Web site (www.csis.org). He has previously served as national security assistant to Senator John McCain of the Senate Armed Services Committee, as director of intelligence assessment in the Office of the Secretary of Defense, as civilian assistant to the deputy secretary of defense, and as director of policy and planning for resource applications in the Department of Energy. He has also served in numerous other government positions, including in the State Department and on NATO International Staff, and he has had numerous foreign assignments, including posts in Lebanon, Egypt, and Iran, with extensive work in Saudi Arabia and the Gulf.

Cordesman is the author of more than 20 books, including a four-volume series on the lessons of modern war. His recent books include *Iraq's Military Capabilities in 2002: A Dynamic Net Assessment* (CSIS, 2002), *Terrorism, Asymmetric Warfare, and Weapons of Mass Destruction* (Praeger/CSIS, 2002), *Cyber-threats, Information Warfare, and Critical Infrastructure Protection* (Praeger/CSIS, 2002), *Strategic Threats and National Missile Defenses* (Praeger/CSIS, 2002), *The Lessons and Non-Lessons of the Air and Missile Campaign in Kosovo* (Praeger, 2001), *Peace and War* (Praeger, 2001), *A Tragedy of Arms* (Praeger, 2001), *Iraq and the War of Sanctions* (Praeger, 2000), and *Iran's Military Forces in Transition* (Praeger, 2000). He has been awarded the Department of Defense Distinguished Service Medal. A former adjunct professor of national security studies at Georgetown University, he has twice been a Wilson Fellow at the Woodrow Wilson International Center for Scholars at the Smithsonian Institution.